# AN UNINHABITED FOREST
## A Play

# AN UNINHABITED FOREST
## A Play

### Pramod Kumar Tripathy

*Translated By*
### Sanjeet Kumar Das

**BLACK EAGLE BOOKS**
Dublin, USA | Bhubaneswar, India

 Black Eagle Books
USA address:
7464 Wisdom Lane
Dublin, OH 43016

India address:
E/312, Trident Galaxy, Kalinga Nagar,
Bhubaneswar-751003, Odisha, India

E-mail: info@blackeaglebooks.org
Website: www.blackeaglebooks.org

First International Edition Published by
Black Eagle Books, 2024

**AN UNINHABITED FOREST (A PLAY)**
**by Pramod Kumar Tripathy**

Translated by **Sanjeet Kumar Das**

Original Copyright © **Pramod Kumar Tripathy**
Translation Copyright © **Sanjeet Kumar Das**

All rights reserved. No part of this publication may be reproduced, stored in a retrieval system, or transmitted, in any form or by any means, electronic, mechanical, photocopying, recording or otherwise without the prior permission of the publisher.

Cover & Interior Design: Ezy's Publication

ISBN- 978-1-64560-596-6 (Paperback)
Library of Congress Control Number: 2024948427

Printed in the United States of America

# Author's View

### Story In A Nutshell And Important Points

01. Place : A forest of the Indian Sub-continent
02. Time : Any time before India gets her Independence until the play is staged.
03. Dramatis Personae
    Male Characters : Banshidhar, Babaji, Swadhin, Guruji
    Female Character : Bishakha
    Child Character : Muna/Muni, Boy
    Trees : Sal, Mango, Neem and Tamarind
04. Stagecraft : Mango, Sal, Neem, and tamarind trees are on stage. They can be placed slightly higher than the stage floor on small blocks or sub-stage.
    The artists and the instrumentalists may sit, visibly or half-visibly, near the side screens or in the traditional style of the proscenium theatre; the characters' entry and exit will be from the stage.
    There is no need for the singers since the play focuses on the 'Complete

Theatre', and the characters should sing the song.

The stage props may be real or imaginary, based on the applicational needs and the importance of dramatic viewpoints. The objects may be displaced through mimes.

05. Sound, Voice, and songs

The pronunciation of the sounds and their types in the play are appropriately hinted at. The play's success heavily depends upon the successful production of the echo in Tree-voice, Tree-speech, Tree-cry, Tree-laughter, etc. The directors and the artists will be more careful while the play is staged. So, if the human or machinery voice is not used, Trees as characters will be appropriately justified. For example, the echo in the tree voice, if the Characters articulate such sounds, the acting will be more realistic and entertaining.

The objectives of the play are two-fold: To heighten the sweetness of traditional and modern style in execution and to fulfill our purpose in the successful staging of the play. Hence, the traditional folk instruments are used as far as possible.

Likewise, if a voice is set or tuned for the birdsong in the play from the first to the last, that will be commonly approved for entertainment throughout.

Nursery Rhymes will be sung in the Public School's style. Like other songs, the "Surya Vandana" is also written by me, and its rhythm and flow are modeled on the "*Sri Gopalsahasranāma*".

06. Acting : Four types of acting- body language, dialogue delivery, imitating others, and acting spontaneously- are profoundly displayed to make the play more realistic and appealing to the human senses. The gradual development of acting here in the play is extended from the traditional Greek model to modern rituals and is suitably garlanded. This will be continued through dialogue delivery and movements. The trees act primarily and are engaged in conversation (through dialogues) with the characters. Sometimes, they do movements such as throwing some fruits, shedding a branch, and their confinement to entry and exit only. They are engrossed in discussion with Banshidhar and Bishakha, and in the presence of others, they stay calm

and quiet, motionless, and become dumb. They also talk to each other in others' presence, which these two can't hear. Banshidhar is here treated or imagined as a dedicated soul to Nature, and Bishakha is his companion soul.

The trees can change their places in the public's front. Nothing is hidden from the public perception. So, while the trees move and Banshidhar grows old, there is no need to turn the stage light off. There should be equidistance between the trees at the time of trees' movement. The unique style is logically feasible but different from free play (Open theatre).

There is no restriction of entry and exit, as the forest does not have inside and outside.

| | | | |
|---|---|---|---|
| 07. | Costumes | : | Wearing costumes are based on the characters. Banshidhar wears a white *dhoti* and a vest and holds a saffron towel. Bishakha wears a deep green saree. Other characters will dress themselves with character-based get-ups. Swadhin with Banshidhar will wear a dhoti, a vest initially, and a suit and shirt later. |
| 08. | My views | : | What's after the folk play/theatre? Nothing is possible without folk |

play in the era after folk play because any thought or idea will contradict the art of play in the Folk Play's aftermath.

In the name of experimental plays with different 'isms', the playwrights defiled our state's public taste and interest for many years. We consider the layman's more profound knowledge and the reaction of the theatres dedicated to entertaining and educating the audience. *An Uninhabited Forest* folk play is designed in the style of *Panchatantra* fantasy.

Big Brothers of our Odia Culture may treat me and my writing as 'untouchable' and let them say so. The contractors and the businessmen may say this is 'useless' and let them say so. I am sure and know well that our audience was not contractors, big brothers, or brokers; they aren't, and they won't be. Thus, 'play/drama' was and will be in the future.

**Prof. Pramod Kumar Tripathy**
*Deulasahi, Ward No: 09*
*Paripada, Mayurbhanja, Odisha, Pin- 757001*

## A True Soul/Mind Needed

For the storytellers of our time, being a simple propagator of only social or political agenda is not enough. Like the great seers of all ages, they should try their best to hypnotize their audience entirely by their creative endeavour. An actual sublime work always brings happiness to its readers and releases them into an imaginary but magical world.

I am one of those who create fantasies in the name of literature. I am one of that group. There is no hesitation on my side to accept this. That literature is capable enough to generate new viewpoints and to open new avenues and horizons.

The pessimism of creative people is not degrading. It is the most awareness for man's freedom, while creative individuals always search for the universal but eternal truth and essence of humanism.

One day, this man's lunacy hurt humanity most; as a son of that race, I must undoubtedly think about the future's danger that is nearing. I have been disappointed sometimes while searching for the path.

**Isaac Bashevis Singer**
*The Nobel Prize in Literature 1978*

## A Forest Needed

Is there any forest where no human beings reside? There may be.

Is there any forest where trees can talk, sing, listen to, laugh, cry, and offer fruits sensing one's mind? There may be.

Maybe, hearing the human's footsteps, they will be silent, or else they will be quiet by the stroke of an axe.

Had they had wings, the trees would have flown miles over miles, but had they had the wings, what would human beings have done? There would not have been any civilization, society, or exploitation.

To the continuous exploitation, indecisive harassment, and plundering, the infinite number of documents of man's materialistic greed in the name of civilization, religion, party politics, and dumb witness is the forest.

Forest is the cornerstone of human civilization.

I have never seen such a tree. It may happen so that the trees may not talk to me. So, imagining such a play through direct experience may not be expected.

In contemporary society, and the decline derived from that, the languor of defeat is created in the human mind. Very mysteriously, an opposite idea is made: "Had it been so, what would have happened!" To the artist, conscious of the situational needs, this type of idea and whim is necessary, for there is the hope that, maybe, the literature created out of this will make the people aware of, and the human civilization may sustain from the forthcoming disaster/apocalypse.

**Prof. Pramod Kumar Tripathy**
Deulasahi, Ward No: 09
Paripada, Mayurbhanja,
Odisha, Pin- 757001

# Translator's View

A professor of English, Pramod Kumar Tripathy is one of the leading playwrights of modern Odia literature. I have translated his Odisha Sangeet Natak Akademi Award 1994-winning play *Jeun Banastare Manisha Nahin* into English as *An Uninhabited Forest*. According to him, the whole world is like a forest where we are all the inhabitants but without humanity. Governed by our whims and urges, we ignore others' growth. We exploit the entire plant and animal kingdom for comfort and happiness. We forget our duty and responsibility towards other species in the environment. Man's conspiracy of looting has made them numb and quiet. The dramatist has made us aware of the contemporary world we live in now: "If we don't take it seriously, we will not only harm us, but also our future generation." The sooner we give up our parasitic approach to life and are determined to work hard, the better we live in the principle of coexistence. The symbiotic nature of human life with the environment is the clarion call of the post-modern world. The excessive exploitation of Nature brings hazardous consequences to the world. The cause for this is human greed. This solipsistic attitude of this race becomes detrimental to other species' life in the world.

In this geological age of the Anthropocene, man's excessive interference with Nature has derailed the ecosystem. Thus, the natural outcome is climate change, which we face nowadays. This play is a warning message to befriending with Nature.

If we don't protect the environment, we will perish soon. There will be no question of sustainable development. Our erstwhile animistic tradition, as prescribed in the scriptural texts, was indeed vital now. Nature came first before human civilization formed. Looking at God's plenty in Nature, humans settled their communities and governed life with cultural codes and norms. Then, the people thought of 'religion/dharma/righteousness' positively. The dharma closely guards us regarding what we should and should not do. We shouldn't think of Nature as a 'permanent giver' unconditionally and unquestionably, but we must try our best to protect it for us and future generations. Nature fulfills our basic needs.

The main protagonist, Banshidhar, is a friend of Nature. He accompanies his wife Vishakha to stay in the forest. Later, they are blessed with a son, Swadhin, who is utterly opposite to them and revolutionary while growing up. Banshidhar and his wife want to lead a peaceful life in the serene, sublime lap of the environment, while his son wants to move away from Nature and join the society/ city to relish better comfort. His son's name is Swadhin, for his birth on 15 August 1947, the day India got her independence. After he joined the group of the ruffians led by Guruji, his name was also codified as 1947.

The play's plot hints at some incidents of the British rule of India and how they exploited and tortured the Indians in the motherland. Some incidents after India's independence are also indirectly referred to. The goons' gang is led by Guruji, who has a colonial bent of mind after the Britishers depart from the country, spreading violence and terror. The gang members are named by numbers, such as 1984 (child character Muna) and 1947 (Swadhin). The other two years, 1965 and 1971, are also mentioned. The years 1965 and 1971 remind us of the Indo-Pakistani wars, respectively. Violence erupted all over India in 1984 by the Sikhs. Those who join the goons' gang are numbered. They metaphorically stand for spreading violence. Guruji was the Gang leader of the group. These Naxalites have kidnapped the kid Muna from the Public School and have named them 1984, which he strongly opposes.

Babaji is a religious swindler who cheats the innocent mob. In contrast, the characters Mango, Neem, Sal, and Tamarind make Banshidhar aware of working instead of sitting idly with a moral lesson:

Tree-Song : Nobody sits idly, nobody requests,
Nobody begs for alms,
One who works standing here,
He relishes the fruit.
Brother, you do work and stand up,
Work hard until you breathe last,
You will enjoy a good result.

When the ungrateful terrorists move to cut down the trees, the dialogues among the trees matter are as follows:

Babaji : Then, Let Lord Ganesh be invoked first…Delay is dangerous. Isn't it?
[All three move to the tree that Muna clasps.]

Sal : Let them chop me first; you live, Mango, because you are the king of fruits.

Mango : Let them chop me first; you live, Neem, because you are the king of medicines.

| | | |
|---|---|---|
| Neem | : | Let them chop me first; you live, Tamarind, because you benefit all. |
| Tamarind | : | Let them chop me first; you live, Sal, because you are the tallest tree for which the forest exists. |

Banshidhar treats Babaji, Guruji, and his son Swadhin as parasites and locusts. It tells us about the evolutionary development of the Earth.

| | | |
|---|---|---|
| Banshidhar | : | Locusts! Parasites!! First forest, then human beings, then party, then dharma. Go to that forest where I am not present…Banshidhar is not there…humans are not there. (Shaking the *maśāl*/light) Go now… |
| Banshidhar | : | I am human, like you. They were vultures. Come to me, my dear. |
| Muna | : | I? |
| Banshidhar | : | (Showing the light/torch) Continue burning the light. When you can't work, you will hand it over to your son only for light. You won't listen to others' flattery or coaxing. Their words may be like the nectar, but being an ascetic and a politician, they will exploit others…yours, mine… (showing to the trees) theirs… (seeing, touching) much blood dripped, no more blood will drip… |
| Muna | : | I will go home, Sir. |
| Banshidhar | : | Make home to the forest, my child, but forest to the home… (handing the torch/light with a long stick |

|  |  |
|---|---|
|  | over to Muna) You watch here... holding the *maśāl*... (He was going.) |
| Muna | : Sir! Leaving me alone, you... |
| Banshidhar | : No, don't say alone... (showing the trees) Rama Kaka, Shama Bhai, Nani, and this Bhai are all with you. Be friends with them; they will talk to you, they will sing for you, they will help you in your sorrows and happiness, and the birds will also return to their nests here. |
| Muna | : But where are you going, Sir? |

Banshidhar understood the philosophy of life well. We live happily because the environment exists. If it is lost, we won't live. As an heir, he has chosen Muna instead of his son Swadhin to protect the environment.

By scripting this play based on 'deep ecology', the dramatist tries to revive the theatre lovers' interest in watching the plays on stage again, as they have been away from the theatres long before being obsessed with experimental plays. He introduced folk elements and songs to entertain the audience and taught them to be conscious of their rich culture and vitality through didacticism.

It is an eco-centric play but not anthropocentric. The playwright has denied the cultural influence over Nature through characters like Banshidhar and Muna. Man's supremacy is denigrated. He recommends a peaceful life and stands firmly against the hypocritical, bustling city life. Our harmonious relationship with Nature can bless us with heavenly bliss and for the rest of our succeeding generations. Banshidhar tells his wife, "I will play the flute, the birds will sing, and you will dance. All of us will stay together and enjoy life here.

The playwright hints at the generation gap between the father Banshidhar and son Swadhin, which is a contemporary problem.

While translating the Odia play of the playwright into English, the rules of equivalence and faithfulness between the Odia language and the target language, English, are carefully considered. I came across some natural shifts. I have translated this text into English using language as lucid as possible for a better understanding of the commoners to have a grip on the aesthetic beauty of the regional language. Some collocational expressions of the source language are with glosses in parentheses in translation.

I want to thank the playwright Pramod Kumar Tripathy's family members, especially his wife, Dr Ushasi Mishra Madam, for believing in me translating this Odia play into English here. I would also like to thank Dr Ganesh Prasad Sahu for helping me select the text for the English rendition.

I convey my heartfelt gratitude to Satya Pattanaik, the director of Black Eagle Books, U.S.A., and Sri Ashok Parida of the publishing house for their kind consent and timely action in publishing the work of art on time.

**SANJEET KUMAR DAS**

# A Critical Appraisal

Pramod Kumar Tripathy (1956-2012) was a successful playwright of the postmodern era after 1980. Trained in English literature, he closely associated with the dramaturgical world and created his name and identity. A professor, he has understood well what postmodernism is. Thus, he successfully founded his literary aura by writing plays in the Odia language and connected himself with Odia readers and audiences. Apart from writing Odia plays, he sponsored Rourkela Loka Natak Mahotsav and other theatre groups. His plays were staged frequently in Rourkela, Sambalpur, Bargarh, and Baripada. His notable plays include *Chau Natak, Dwitiya Mrutyu, Rajakiya, Kalapurusha, Jathara, Hanu Upadraba Sambad, Sanbalua, and Ramachandra Pheriasa. Cancer, Nishanta, Partha, Ankurodgama, Shuna Pariksha Dandadhari, Jeun Banastare Manusha Nahin, Gotie Bula Kukurara Janma Brutanta* etc. Though so many plays were staged, some are yet to be staged.

The play "An Uninhabited Forest" is considered an important Odia play. It received the **Odisha Sangeet Natak Akademi Award** in 1994 and was published in book form in 1999. Contemporary issues are addressed with the injunction of the Imaginary and Folk Theatre style. Not being influenced by Western tradition, the writer Pramod Tripathy used play to preserve India's historical sense and tradition. The play "An Uninhabited Forest" can be studied multi-dimensionally. The play deals with concepts like civilization, the gradual development of human culture, and the formation of family, society, and state issues from Lord Shiva and Parvati. So, the writer prescribes that the forest comes first on the earth, then man, then religious groups and then political or communal parties in due course. But it is marked that the party controls dharma (religion), religion to human beings, people control/ruin the forest or environment. The writer in this play allegorically represents the historical development of human civilization. Protecting the environment and the human-environ symbiotic relationship are interlaced through characters like the Mango Tree, Tamarind Tree, Sal Tree, Neem Tree, and Banshidhar. The trees have taught Banshidhar the formula or principle of how to live in society. But people gradually lead indisciplined lives and destroy the environment. The play also incorporates the characters of religious and political groups like Babaji and Guruji, who believe in spreading violence and terror. These people guide the country's youth on the path of degeneration in the post-independent era. The man who does not understand the true meaning of 'Independence' destabilizes the society and ruins the country. The structure of the play is entirely new. It has been successfully staged without acts and scenes. The play sheds light on history, politics, religion, and the protection of the environment. The play is essential for its structural composition and stands conspicuous from its contemporary writers' works of art. Preserving culture, humanity, patriotism, and a balanced relationship between humans and the environment can be beautifully thought of in a country like India. Otherwise, without humanity, family, society, and the state, we would be like a forest, a habitat for animals.

**Dr. Ganesh Prasad Sahu**
Assistant Professor
Department of Odia Language and Literature
Central University of Odisha, Koraput

# An Uninhabited Forest

[A neat and clean place in the dense forest is chosen. It's lush green everywhere. No human beings have entered the forest.

The trees, creepers, and hilly brooks are displayed on the cyclorama. Four trees are visible to the audience on the stage. They are the different characters of the play. The wind's serenade is heard along with the babbling brook and intermittently listened to the wild creatures' loud calls (In human language, 'wild') and birds' chirping. When the wind blows reasonably higher than the average speed, the tops of the trees shake.

The setting of the play is a portion of the Indian subcontinent.

Time is of Pre-independent India.

A few minutes before the main curtain is raised, the following song is heard with traditional instrument music:

"Have you ever seen a forest where no human beings reside?"

The stanza is echoed in the chorus and musical accompaniment at different places in the play. The curtain is raised when the music is on, and a choric song is heard as the trees and the characters sing in unison.]

Song : You have created the whole world,
You have created us—

We bow our heads down a thousand times,
accept our obeisance.
You have given the life-wind in the sky,
water in the river.
Beneath our feet, the soil, sunlight
You have bestowed the world with energy.
Bending our head a thousand times,
We pledge and promise you,
The whole world will go green,
We will help it go green.
[When the last line, "We will help it go green" wanes, gets repeated and echoed, in the vicinity is heard someone's entry and breathing at the spot. The trees converse in apprehension.]

| | | |
|---|---|---|
| Sal Tree | : | Can you hear, Mango? |
| Mango Tree | : | Yes, my buddy. Perhaps, someone is coming! |
| Neem Tree | : | Is he coming at this side? |
| Tamarind Tree | : | Is it not the king tiger? |
| Mango | : | The tiger king won't breathe like this! |
| Neem | : | O Tamarind! It seems to be a monkey. |
| Tamarind | : | How come that rascal monkey reached here? It will go and jump on me. Hello, what's the matter? No, my wish! It will jump, trample, scratch, and bruise my hands and face. |
| Sal | : | Listen to me…you all listen to me…<br>[In the serene forest, there is a rustling noise.] |

| | | |
|---|---|---|
| Tamarind | : | Who can it be, Sal? |
| Mango | : | You are the tallest of us. Try to see it closely. |
| Sal | : | (Having seen) I can't understand. I have never heard this type of sound in my life. |
| Neem | : | Has God sent a new animal to the forest (us)? |

[When the trees interact, they will act like human characters. While moving from one place to another, they must take their legs off the ground, as if the tree's trunk changes its place. The voices and songs of the trees will be heard from the background. After all, the distribution is expected to be open and traditional. Acting and dialogue delivery are of human style; instead, they are unique and special, and the style of the tree is different. As there is no restriction on prosaic or poetic style of expression, the conversational dialogues may be lyrical, prosaic or a combination of the two. The timid Banshidhar comes surreptitiously. Loneliness has given him the courage to stand up for a moment. Only the two eyes stare at the external surroundings from the body covered with a worn-out dirty shawl. Feeling safe and assured, he removes the shawl from his face. When he looks around, the trees converse.]

| | | |
|---|---|---|
| Sal | : | He is looking at me. |
| Mango | : | He is looking at me. |
| Neem | : | He is looking at me. |
| Tamarind | : | He is looking at me. |

[Banshidhar is startled by the rustling sound on the ground.]

| | | |
|---|---|---|
| Mango | : | Two legs |
| Tamarind | : | Two hands |
| Neem | : | No horns |
| Sal | : | No tail |
| Banshidhar | : | Who? |

[The word "Who?" spreads from tree to tree.]

Banshidhar : Oh, my voice! (Loudly) Who?

[The word is again echoed: "Who?"]

Banshidhar : (Loudly) Banshidhar.

[There is an echo of 'Banshidhar'... 'Banshidhar']

Banshidhar : Nobody is here. This forest is far away from the city. Nobody is here. The surroundings are clean, beautiful, charming and entertaining. Banshidhar can live here, forgetting his past. Banshidhar, you stay here and forget your past, house verandah, village courtyard, grain yard...and your wife...

Banshidhar's tone : Do you remember your wife?

[This voice is different from the trees' voice and of human beings.]

Banshidhar : Yes, who else is mine? My parents, my brothers, and my sisters are in the heavenly abode.

| | | |
|---|---|---|
| Banshidhar's tone | : | How often do you remember, Banshidhar? |
| Banshidhar | : | How can I fathom? |
| Banshidhar's tone | : | How could the white Sepoys have released you? You didn't touch their feet. |
| Banshidhar | : | I was right. What he could have done to me was right but to my Lalita... [A cry of distress in a lady's voice: "No...no...leave me...my husband... ah."] |
| Banshidhar | : | (Slip of tongue) Lalita! [The lady's voice gets diminished.] |
| Banshidhar's tone | : | Hello, why do you behave like this? This is a forest! |
| Banshidhar | : | They fastened me to the pillar raised in the house courtyard and in front of my eyes... |
| Banshidhar's tone | : | They are the government servants! What else could they have done? How will they live if they don't execute government orders? They are all traitors of the traitors' dynasty. |
| Banshidhar | : | It's a lie. It is the white people's lie. Still, then, they have driven away me from my land. They had ostracized me, beating the drums. What fault had I committed, Banshidhar? This is because I had spoken the truth. |
| Banshidhar's tone | : | Leave it. Let bygone be bygone. Forget that... |
| Banshidhar | : | Be determined, Mind! Forget everything. |

| | |
|---|---|
| Banshidhar's tone : | Look to the future. |
| Banshidhar : | He is looking ahead. |
| Banshidhar's tone : | The politicians say the green future lies ahead. |
| Banshidhar : | They are telling. |
| Banshidhar's tone : | Anything more? |
| Banshidhar : | I am hungry; what will I eat? I am thirsty; what will I drink? (Yawning) I am sleepy; where will I sleep? Steamed rice, cold water, soft bed! No chance of getting here! |
| Banshidhar's tone : | If you think, you will get everything here.<br>[Banshidhar becomes happy looking around.] |
| Sal : | He is talking. |
| Mango : | To Himself |
| Neem : | He is smiling. |
| Tamarind : | To Himself |
| Banshidhar : | Who? Nobody is here. Alas! What big fruits that tree has been with! Sweet and juicy fruits!<br>[He tries to pluck the fruits, jumping and fails. The boughs of the trees rise higher and higher. He is thrown down.] |
| Banshidhar : | Oh, here, there is no wind or storm. How does the bough go upward when I raise my hands to pluck the fruits?<br>[He tries for the second time and gets failed.] |
| Banshidhar : | Well! If I pelt a stone, the fruits will be piled on the ground...I am pelting |

## An Uninhabited Forest | 27

| | | |
|---|---|---|
| | | now (He searches for the pebbles.) |
| Mango | : | (Terrified) He tells to pelt stones. |
| Neem | : | Only saying! |
| Banshidhar | : | (Getting the stone) This one is good. [When he picks up the stone from the ground and raises it to throw, he hears the tree cry. He stops for a while without getting the source of the cry. There is no cry. When he tries to pelt again, he hears the tree cry.] |
| Banshidhar | : | This is strange! Very amazing! Who is here? [There is an echo in the tree's tone: who? Who?] |
| Banshidhar | : | Hello. Who's crying here? (Taking a breath) Who is crying here in this wild and dense forest? |
| Mango | : | I am the tree. |
| Banshidhar | : | Tree? |
| Mango | : | Yes, I am. |
| Banshidhar | : | (Smiling) Tree? Again crying? Unbelievable! |
| Mango | : | I am crying. |
| Banshidhar | : | Oh, yes! Many trees are here; who's crying? [All the four trees shake simultaneously.] |
| Trees | : | We are all crying. |
| Banshidhar | : | You are talking, crying… (having seen the backside of trees) nobody is here. Why will the trees cry? How? |
| Mango | : | Will you pelt stones at me? |
| Banshidhar | : | What! |

| | | |
|---|---|---|
| Mango | : | A stone is in your hands. I am afraid of that. |
| Banshidhar | : | I threw it. I won't pelt at you.<br>[All the four trees shake themselves simultaneously.] |
| Banshidhar | : | Are you happy? Don't be afraid of me. |
| Mango | : | What kind of animal are you? |
| Banshidhar | : | I am... an animal? |
| Mango | : | Who are you? Who? |
| Banshidhar | : | I am Banshidhar, hailing from Jagannathapur. |
| Sal | : | Who are you? Who? |
| Banshidhar | : | I am the son of Gangadhar Nayak. Now, I am unemployed. |
| Neem | : | Who are you? Who? |
| Banshidhar | : | I am Lalita's husband. The British Government...I was a good citizen; now, I am in a foreign land. |
| Tamarind | : | Who are you? Who? |
| Banshidhar | : | (Out of annoyance) Oh, I am a human being. Do you understand?<br>[Echo in the tree's tone: 'Human being'... 'Human being'] |
| Banshidhar | : | I am a human being. I should live in the city. I should live in society. For my misfortune, I have come here. They didn't listen to me. |
| Sal | : | Do all listen to you? |
| Banshidhar | : | Why won't they hear me? I am a human being. |
| Neem | : | Are you more powerful than the tiger-king? |
| Banshidhar | : | (Smiling) Where is tiger? where am I? |

## An Uninhabited Forest | 29

|  |  |  |
|---|---|---|
|  |  | There is no comparison between us. He listens to me. |
| Tamarind | : | (shaking) Does the tiger-king listen to you? |
| Banshidhar | : | Why not? |
| Mango | : | How? You don't have claws, big teeth, or red eyes! |
| Banshidhar | : | I have all these. I am human! Won't it listen to me? |
| Mango | : | But how? |
| Banshidhar | : | If I get an opportunity to cheat the tiger, assaulting it from the backside, I will take it to society. |
| Sal | : | You take? What does he do there? |
| Banshidhar | : | It is no longer a king there! It dances there in the circus or the zoo. |
| Neem | : | Tiger-king? |
| Tamarind | : | Does he dance there? |
| Mango | : | How does he dance there, Man? |
| Banshidhar | : | (Dancing) Like this. |
| Trees | : | Alas! |

[Banshidhar displays a sample of bear-dance. The trees smile, nodding their tops.]

| Banshidhar | : | Can you laugh? |
| Sal | : | We are born for that- we smile and make others smile. |

[Banshidhar is getting tired and has sat down. The trees stop their smiling.]

| Neem | : | What happened to you, Man? |
| Banshidhar | : | I am tired. |
| Sal | : | Tired? What's that? |
| Banshidhar | : | I have no energy right now. |

| | | |
|---|---|---|
| Trees | : | Okay! |
| Banshidhar | : | I had my food last a few days ago. As I have danced before you for a moment, I am exhausted…I am hungry now. |
| Mango | : | Hungry? |
| Banshidhar | : | I am also thirsty. |
| Tamarind | : | Thirsty? |
| Banshidhar | : | I must take something to my stomach…food and liquid… |
| Sal | : | You stand up, Man. |
| Banshidhar | : | I can't. |
| Sal | : | You are alive, but you can't. |
| Banshidhar | : | If I don't take anything, how can I… |
| Mango | : | Please have something. |
| Banshidhar | : | (Happily) I will eat…yes, I will eat. (picking up stones) I will eat mango. |
| Mango | : | Man! |
| Banshidhar | : | I was making the same mistake for the second time. (Throwing down the stone) Oh, tree! Give me fruits. |
| Mango | : | No |
| Banshidhar | : | If not mango, I can have tamarind or neem. |
| Neem & Tamarind | : | No |
| Banshidhar | : | (Requesting) I am hungry now… please give me fruits. |
| Sal | : | See, buddy! Human beings surrender for food. |
| Mango | : | This does not happen in our land. |
| Banshidhar | : | What will Banshidhar do here? When I am throwing stones at you, you are angry. When I beg for food, you laugh. Tree, give me food, or else I will die. |

| | | |
|---|---|---|
| Trees | : | No...no...no |
| Banshidhar | : | (Out of hunger, anger, and irritation) Why not? |
| Sal | : | Because... |

[In traditional style, the chorus of tree-song]

| | | |
|---|---|---|
| Song | : | Nobody sits idly, nobody requests, Nobody begs for alms, One who works standing here, He relishes the fruit. Brother, you do work and stand up, Work hard until you breathe last, You will enjoy life well. |

[The last stanza, 'Work hard until you breathe last, You will enjoy the good result.' The trees slow down soon.]

| | | |
|---|---|---|
| Banshidhar | : | Yes...yes...I will work. [He stands up.] |

[The trees oscillate.]

| | | |
|---|---|---|
| Banshidhar | : | Hold on...Tell me one thing, tree. You are weighed down with fruits. If you give me some, what loss will you bear? |
| Mango | : | We won't lose anything, but you will. |
| Banshidhar | : | If I get it, how will I bear the loss? Tell me now? |
| Mango | : | You will be accustomed to begging. Like you, others will also start begging all over the state. You will ask for alms throughout the market. Your state will be considered poor. Your state will be declared as the State of Beggars. |

| | | |
|---|---|---|
| Banshidhar's Tone: | | Your successors in the family will also be beggars. |
| Banshidhar | : | (Being terrified) No…no…no…I won't let them do that. Gandhiji says, stand on your legs. I will stand myself. After the British Government leaves, my family members will also stand independently: they will work hard and eat. |
| Sal | : | This is precisely what we want. |
| Banshidhar | : | Tree, you say what I can do. (To Mango) hello…hello…why are you trembling? |
| Mango | : | My body itches. |
| Banshidhar | : | You are a tree. (smiling) Again, your body is itching. |
| Mango | : | You see! The creepers/parasites are sucking me. |
| Banshidhar | : | Oh! It is like the lice on the human head. |
| Mango | : | They don't have any work, only sucking me and disturbing me. Oh! You remove them from my body. |
| Banshidhar | : | I am driving them away from you, as the British Government is in our country.<br>[Banshidhar removes some creepers from the Mango Tree.] |
| Mango | : | (Being relaxed) Oh! |
| Banshidhar | : | They are also found in our areas/country but in different forms. |
| Neem | : | Yes, they are also human beings. |
| Banshidhar | : | Yes, they are, but not like me. They |

|  |  |
|---|---|
| | look like me externally but are different internally. |
| Tamarind | : Are they human beings? |
| Banshidhar | : (Singing) |
| | Some are attendants; some are flatterers. |
| | Some are landlords; some are businessmen. |
| | Some follow, some flatter, |
| | Say 'sir', 'sir' to the King, the Watchmen. |
| Trees | : (maintaining rhythm) Say 'sir', 'sir' to the King, the Watchmen. |
| Banshidhar | : Some, placed in the monastery, chant God's name, |
| | Some worship the British Government on stage. |
| Trees | : (maintaining rhythm) Some worship the British Government on stage. |
| Banshidhar | : I will uproot them all. |
| | [Smashing the creepers in their hands, he throws them away.] |
| Mango | : Well, you work like this, Man. We will provide you with food and open this country's storeroom. Take…take…take… |
| | [Ripe fruits fall on the ground from the grown-up trees and on Banshidhar's body. Happily, Banshidhar gathers the fruits.] |
| Banshidhar's tone | : I will work…I will eat; I will work…I will eat. I will uproot the parasites. Now and in the future. Oh, Brook! |

|   |   |
|---|---|
| | I will clean your bank and bed. Will you give me water? [The brook babbles like the anklets of a nubile.] |
| Banshidhar | : What more do I need, Lord? I am satisfied. [Banshidhar eats fruits in the special light. By the time the normal lights are on, Banshidhar releases acid breath happily.] |
| Tamarind | : Have you had more than the usual, Man? |
| Banshidhar | : (releasing acid breath) I had not eaten anything for the last two days, tree. So, Oh, what a sleep! |
| Neem | : Can the animals sleep, Man? |
| Banshidhar | : (Releasing acid air) There is shade in the lower portion of the Sal tree. Banshidhar tries to sleep there, clearing that portion and spreading a bedsheet. Evening sets in gradually. Banshidhar couldn't sleep. |
| Mango | : Can't you sleep, Man? |
| Sal | : Sing songs and sleep. |
| Banshidhar | : I am feeling awkward. I know how to play the flute, but I am not interested. (Being disappointed) That's not with me now. |
| Tamarind | : Wait a while; our male and female singers will reach here. |
| Banshidhar | : (Sitting) Your male and female singers? |
| Neem | : The birds will return to their nests. They will help you sleep by singing. |

An Uninhabited Forest | 35

|  |  |
|---|---|
|  | [The bird chirping is heard. Banshidhar tries to sleep again.] |
| Song | : *Nida māusī, nida māusī*! (A good fairy who induces sleep in someone.) <br> On which branch are you sitting? <br> *Nida māusī, nida māusī*! <br> Come down for a while to the ground. <br> [Banshidhar flips his side while sleeping.] |
| Song | : *Nida māusī, nida māusī*! <br> I can neither sleep nor sit. <br> *Nida māusī, nida māusī*! <br> Say why you do pretend so much, <br> Enter (induce sleep to) the guest's eyes. <br> [Birdsong diminishes. Banshidhar gets up from bed.] |
| Banshidhar's Tone | : Do you remember your wife? |
| Banshidhar | : Yes, who else does live with me? My parents and my sisters are no longer in this world. |
| Banshidhar's Tone | : How much do you remember her? |
| Banshidhar | : How can I say? (To the trees) How can I fathom my love for her? (To the birds) How can I fathom my love for her? (Shouting) I can't sleep. <br> [The sound 'No' gets echoed from tree to tree.] |
| Trees | : What happened? <br> [When the trees bend, the birds get up in their nest and start twittering.] |
| Banshidhar | : Calm down, calm down, please. (Addressing to all) I am not |

determined to rest peacefully or sleep well. I recollect all those scenes. The British (White) Sepoys, one after one, to my wife in front of my eyes...her distressed cry is heard from the city to the forest. I don't know whether she is alive or dead, my friend. If she were still alive, what would she be doing? I was driven away from the village, poked at the gunpoint and beaten severely. I have married her; I will be with her in her sorrows and happiness. If she were alive, she would wait for me, hint at me, and shed her tears sleeplessly...no, I will go, I will go, I will go; I will bring her and keep her with me here. The British Government can›t know this that both husband and wife should stay together. We will live together and die together.

| | | |
|---|---|---|
| Sal | : | Is she a human being? |
| Banshidhar | : | Yes, marriages are held between human beings. |
| Mango | : | She is like you, Man? |
| Banshidhar | : | Yes, she is but female. |
| Neem | : | Does she eat, drink, and sleep like you? |
| Banshidhar | : | Don›t worry, Trees. We will share what you will give us. We will neither pelt stones at you nor disturb you all. Again...she will work like me...she will work...she will eat. |
| Tamarind | : | Will she eat what you eat? |

| | |
|---|---|
| Banshidhar | : Tamarind! When the white sepoys entered my house, my wife was eating tamarind. |
| Tamarind | : After that? |
| Banshidhar | : What happened next? Before I knew that, I was severely beaten... (Banshidhar shows his back. The trees show sympathy.) |
| Trees | : Alas...alas... evil! |
| Banshidhar | : My sores need time to recover completely. Still, then, I will go and assure you that, by next morning, I will be back. |
| | [The birds scream.] |
| Banshidhar | : Birds, you won't go anywhere. We will return. You will sing; I will play my flute while she dances. Now? No, I am not with a flute now. I have placed it in the niche of my bedroom's wall. It will be there. Had I been with a gun, the British Government would have snatched it away from us. That is not fit for the flute. I will bring that...I will go and come back. I and my Lalita, my flute...will come back... (Seeking permission) ...can I go now, my friend? |
| | [The wind's music, bird's chirping, and then the tree-song are on.] |
| Song | : Hello, Brother Man! Reach your community soon. Happy journey! Please, return to the forest, accompanying your wife. |

[As earlier, Banshidhar covers his body with the shawl and meets the trees, and they shake themselves.]

Song : A flute you will bring, here is the drum,
Birds will sing songs; we all will enjoy life.

[As earlier, Banshidhar nods and leaves the place secretly.]

Song : We will stay happily in the forest; all are equal here,
We will make the earth go green with all our efforts.

[Darkness sets in slowly, and the stage lights are off and turned on again; the morning appears after removing the night's darkness. The golden ray of the rising sun kisses the forest land.]

Song : Have you seen a forest, brother,
Where no human beings ever reside?

[It is morning when the stage lights are entirely on. Banshidhar enters with a large bag in his hands. His dresses-*dhoti*, vest, and a towel-now the shawl seems slightly washed. He is pleased and comes dancing and playing the flutes.]

Banshidhar : (Calling) Come, you come... (To the trees, announcing) we have come.

[The trees have shaken their heads.]

Banshidhar : Haven't I told you that we will return? But we were late. By the time I reached my village, my Lalita had committed suicide (by hanging herself with a rope), not bearing the insult. She lost her pregnancy. I felt very sorry. Well, there is the good news. I have met the leader of our community. He says, "Gandhiji has told that the Brits will return to London, this time quitting our country." The women like Lalita won't commit suicide nowadays.

| | | |
|---|---|---|
| Sal | : | Have you come alone? |
| Banshidhar | : | No…no…not alone… (hey, come…) |
| Mango | : | Who is she, Man? |
| Banshidhar | : | Bishakha |
| Neem | : | Is she a human being? |
| Banshidhar | : | Ouch! She was my sister-in-law, but now she is my wife. |
| Tamarind | : | Is she also a human being? |
| Banshidhar | : | She is a human but female. |
| Mango | : | What have you held in your hands? |
| Banshidhar | : | This is a bag. |
| Neem | : | What have you kept in that bag? |
| Banshidhar | : | Dhoti, vest, towel and flute |
| Banshidhar's tone | : | Don't speak the truth, Banshidhar. |
| Banshidhar | : | I have never told any lies, and that's why I suffer. |
| Banshidhar's tone | : | Avoid this… pretend… otherwise, they won't offer you fruits and shade; brook won't provide you water; the birds won't sing for you, Banshidhar. |
| Banshidhar | : | Then? |
| Banshidhar's tone | : | Don't speak the truth or tell a lie; do acting. |
| Tamarind | : | Is there anything else in that bag? |

| | | |
|---|---|---|
| Banshidhar | : | Hold on…You need not know what else I am with, Tree. I am poor; what else could I have? (Calling) Hey, O Bishakha, please come! |
| Bishakha | : | (From the background) Alas! Where are you taking me? |
| Banshidhar | : | Come with me to see a beautiful spot. [Banshidhar's acting is less natural now than earlier.] |
| Bishakha | : | (Entering) What kind of place is it? [Banshidhar dances happily.] |
| Banshidhar | : | We will stay here only. |
| Bishakha | : | Can I live in this unworthy place? |
| Banshidhar | : | Yes, you can stay with me. This place is ours only. |
| Bishakha | : | There are plenty of places in our village, Jagannathapur. Why will we live under the trees? This is a jungle! |
| Banshidhar | : | If we stay together, this jungle will also be Jagannathapur. |
| Bishakha | : | People are not here. |
| Banshidhar | : | These trees are good people. |
| Bishakha | : | Are trees people? |
| Banshidhar | : | Though they are not people but behave like people, the Tree-people. |
| Bishakha | : | Your mood has been changed by Sepoy's lathi-charging. |
| Banshidhar | : | I am telling you the fact. I was with these trees only. These trees are far better than the villagers. Each one here is a Gandhi! They will only give fruits, flowers and juice. Hey, that brook has assured me of water. |

An Uninhabited Forest | 41

Bishakha : (Putting a hand on her forehead) What!
Banshidhar : I will play my flute; the birds will sing, and you will dance.
Bishakha : Will I dance in this rough, uneven place?
Banshidhar : Won't the place be made even by our footsteps?
Bishakha : How?
Banshidhar : My great grandfather's grandpa's father had told me when he reached Jagannathpur, it was entirely jungle and full of highlands (mounds of earth). Isn't it normal now?
Bishakha : (Understanding the relationship) Who was telling you?
Banshidhar : His great-grandson's grandson
Bishakha : Maybe-
Banshidhar : Well! While you smile, the world will be smiling.
Bishakha : If there is nothing laughable, how will I laugh? Now, I feel like crying. Hello, my dear! Please tell me where we will live.
Banshidhar : Here only! (He is sweeping the ground.)
Bishakha : What! Here! (Lamenting) O *Nāni* (to the elder sister)! I am married to your husband! He will put me before the tiger. Bringing me to the forest, he tells me to live under trees!
Banshidhar : Alas! What do you mean by 'under the trees'?
Bishakha : Then, is it a 'house'? no...no...
Banshidhar : You are right. Listen to me; I have chalked out a plan.

| | | |
|---|---|---|
| Bishakha | : | What! What have you planned? |
| Banshidhar | : | A plan. My plan is in my bag. You will see how it works at the right time. |
| Bishakha | : | You know when the right time will come. |
| Banshidhar | : | Then listen to me… [Hiding from the trees, he whispers Bishakha and shows her the bag.] |
| Bishakha | : | Is it true? |
| Banshidhar | : | You have seen in your eyes. |
| Bishakha | : | Yes, still then…you say I will do it now. I am hungry now. I would bring a bowl of flattened rice, two bowls of puffed rice, a solid piece of jaggery and a half piece of pickle with me! |
| Banshidhar | : | (Teasing her) I would bring a salted, dried piece of green mango, a slice of ripe mango dried, and a salted, dried fish with me! |
| Bishakha | : | O, yes…you have denied all those and said we will get everything in the new place. |
| Banshidhar | : | Will we get it? (To the Mango Tree) O Tree, give me fruits. |
| Mango | : | (Nodding) Work? |
| Bishaka | : | (Misunderstanding) Alas, what has happened to your throat? |
| Banshidhar | : | (Misunderstanding the question) Am I right…hear…(Testing) O…Bi…Sha…kha… |
| Bishakha | : | O, stop cajoling your love. Say what I will eat…after having food, anything else. |

| | | |
|---|---|---|
| Banshidhar | : | Do you want to have food? Be ready… see, you collect as much as you want… (To the Mango Tree as the guardian) O tree, give me fruits. |
| Mango | : | Work? |
| Bishakha | : | Again, what happened to your throat? |
| Banshidhar | : | (Smiling) Oh! The tree is talking to me. |
| Bishakha | : | You are mad, or else I am. How had my sister been with you for long? |
| Banshidhar | : | Truly speaking, this is Tree's voice. |
| Bishakha | : | Never! |
| Banshidhar | : | These trees can talk and even sing. |
| Bishakha | : | I have been waiting to hear this since I entered this world. |
| Banshidhar | : | Have you ever visited the forest where no human beings reside? |
| Bishakha | : | Are they not ghosts or fiends? |
| Banshidhar | : | Not at all. The trees can talk like us… for this, you should have clean ears. They can talk and gossip among themselves and with human beings, too. |
| Bishakha | : | No one before… |
| Banshidhar | : | If anybody becomes friends with them, and once they believe, they will talk and share their sorrows and happiness, as with me they behave… |
| Bishakha | : | (With widening eyes happily and loudly) …is it true? [Echo in the trees: "True" "True" "True"] |
| Bishakha | : | (Dancing like a girl) Oh my God! |
| Banshidhar | : | Did you hear? |
| Bishakha | : | I have heard the stories from my |

grandma. Now I listen to them talking. (Revolving around) Can they speak to me?

Banshidhar : They can.
Bishakha : They can also sing.
Banshidhar : They can. You can test them. If they become friends with you and talk to you, your life will be great and successful.

[Banshidhar has gone outside.]

Bishakha : How? O, where are you? (To the trees) Hello, my friends…

Song : If humans labour, we will talk to them. Working hard, if they eat, we will dispel their plights.
If humans labour, we will sing songs for them.
If the people walk on the path of justice and righteousness,
*Bhārata* (India) will shine and smile forever.

[When the song ends, Bishakha gets overwhelmed and praises the greatness of the Almighty and says 'Namaskar' to the Earth, the Sky, and the deities of the ten directions.]

Bishakha : O Goddess Baishakhi! O Goddess Barashai! O Goddess Bansatāi! O Goddess Phagunāi! This is your greatness! I have heard here something strange. I am grateful to you! I will work until I die. I will do what you say. I will pick up the dry leaves, smear the cow dung mixed water on the ground, water the plants, worship, and fast.

[The ripe fruits fall on the ground. And on Bishakha's body, too. Banshidhar enters, and seeing the fruits on the ground, he starts dancing. Both garner fruits in great happiness as if they live together and lead their family life. Through special light effects, their family activities are hinted at. Banshidhar plays the flute, the birds chirp, Bishakha dances, and the Trees nod happily. There are hints of Time passing: morning, day, night, and again morning, day, and night. Towards the end, after dancing for a long time, Bishakha tilts down and holds her belly. Banshidhar holds her saying, "Bishakha". Silence pervades there. The stage lights are off.]

[Again, the stage lights are on. The Pregnant Bishakha smears the ground beneath the trees with cow-dung mixed water.]

| | | |
|---|---|---|
| Tamarind | : | Hey, will you take tamarinds? |
| Bishakha | : | (Happily) Yes…yes… (Looking around) Give me… |
| Tamarind | : | If your husband sees, he will be annoyed with me. |
| Bishakha | : | He has gone outside and won't come now. |

| | | |
|---|---|---|
| Tamarind | : | (To the Sal Tree) Can you check whether Manisa bhāi is coming? |
| Sal | : | Nobody comes. Shake your branches now, and she will collect many tamarinds. |
| Tamarind | : | Woman! Take now… |

[A large quantity of tamarinds falls on Bishakha's lap. She gets pleased and thrilled. Widening her eyes, she licks the tamarinds. Banshidhar enters, holding a sapling in his hands.]

| | | |
|---|---|---|
| Banshidhar | : | (Happily) See, Bishakha, you see how our sapling will grow and bear fruits one day. |
| Bishakha | : | (Happily) How plumy and tasty these are! (Putting palms on her belly in pain) How big it is! |
| Banshidhar | : | (looking at her) Again, are you taking tamarind? I denied you earlier. (To the Tamarind Tree) My friendship with you is cut off! |

[Banshidhar, especially Bishakha's behaviour, gradually becomes natural.]

| | | |
|---|---|---|
| Bishakha | : | (Coyly) What could I have eaten? I wouldn't say I like everything. |
| Banshidhar | : | (thinking differently) Like this, nothing was tasty and relishing to your elder sister. She ate tamarind, pickles, and salted, dried pieces of green mango day and night…but the Almighty did not tolerate it. |
| Bishakha | : | Again? But we live happily. |
| Banshidhar | : | What I was telling you is that, if you |

|  |  |
|---|---|
|  | don't eat properly, then (touching her abdomen) what will happen to that unfortunate... |
| Bishakha | : How did you know that it's 'unfortunate'? |
| Banshidhar | : When I touched your belly, it kicked me...that's why... |
| Banshidhar | : Fine! Fine!! |
| Bishakha | : What then? |
| Banshidhar | : (Happily) The Head of our community was right to say Bishakha. |
| Bishakha | : What? |
| Banshidhar | : Can't you hear the fireworks crack? |
| Bishakha | : I am afraid of. |
| Banshidhar | : The 'Age of Fear/Terror' is over. |
| Bishakha | : Over? Why? |
| Banshidhar | : Why? (Reciting happily) Wallago attu fishes diffused brightly in the river, Fig flowers unleashed sweet fragrance, Arrange the funnels and gongs, O my brother! Gandhiji said, 'The British Government left our country.' |
| Bishakha | : Is it true? |
| Banshidhar | : Unlike your elder sister, nobody will poke your belly with a gunpoint this time. Our country got her independence. [The trees nod their heads.] |
| Neem | : Human beings? |
| Banshidhar | : Independence means we are all free from the foreign country's rule or |

|  |  |
|---|---|
|  | dominance, Tree-Brother? When our country is independent, the people of the country are independent.<br>[The fireworks crack heavily.] |
| Bishakha | : (Fearfully)...O, come closer to me... (with pain) I will sleep...(Holding her bundle) Oh my God! |
| Banshidhar | : Why are you afraid of? Ah, silence pervades there. Let's go.<br>[Both of them enter slowly. While returning to their nests, birds scream. Darkness sets in gradually. Amidst the fireworks cracking, Bishakha's labour pain starts. A firework cracks with an explosion than before. Trees question.] |
| Tamarind | : What happened? |
| Background Voice: | "At the stroke of the midnight hour..." |
| Neem | : What happened? |
| Background Voice: | When the world sleeps... |
| Mango | : What happened: |
| Background Voice: | India will awake... |
| Sal | : What happened? |
| Background Voice: | to life and freedom. * |
|  | [Birds flutter their wings.] |
| Tamarind | : The birds are awake now. |
| Neem | : They flutter their wings. |
| Mango | : Won't they desert our land? |
| Sal | : Their parents may fly away, but what about their offspring?<br>[From the background, a newborn baby's uninterrupted cry is heard. The first ray of the morning sun makes |

the forest land golden in colour as if it were the beginning of 'The Golden Age'. Banshidhar enters, dancing happily.]

*[A few minutes before India got her independence at midnight of 14-15 August 1947, on the stage of Constitutional Legislators, it's a portion of Pandit Jawaharlal Nehru's speech.]

Banshidhar : I am blessed with a son, Tree Brother!
Mango : Is he a human?
Banshidhar : (Out of vexation) Can human beings give birth to a monkey?
Sal : Who knows?
Banshidhar : Who knows?
Neem : Trees give birth to trees, birds to birds, animals to animals; human child?
Banshidhar : Exactly like that, human beings give birth to human beings. This child will be a grown-up man later. Now, you hear how he cries like a human child. Like this (Crying) *om...om...aum... aum...aum...aham...aham...aham...*
Tamarind : (Imitating) *om...om...aum...aum... aum...*I can't.
[The Trees imitate Banshidhar till *om... om...aum...aum...aum...*in unison. They can't pronounce '*aham*'. Tree's recitaion]
Trees : *om...om...aum...aum... om...om... aum...aum*
[The forest gets echoed in the 'AUM'

sound. While Banshidhar is crying and imitating, the passing of time is marked by the arrangement of lights. While the 'OM' sound comes down from four to three, from three to two, from two to one, and disappears completely, the baby cries with the sound 'AHAM' sound, and the lights are lit on the stage. Bishakha enters and breastfeeds a three-month-old baby from inside. Her appearance is solemn. The baby is crying.]

Bishakha : No…no…no…
Banshidhar : Why are you making him cry?
Bishakha : (To the baby) no…no… (To Banshidhar) He is not drinking.
Banshidhar : Not drinking? Does he poo and pee?
Bishakha : Yes…(Experiencing) Oh My God! He shivers in the cold.
Banshidhar : Winter has set in…(Touching) cover him… (She covers the baby by taking her shawl off her body.)
Bishakha : The winter has set in here for a long time. What will we do? (To the baby) Oh, my child, my wealth! Take…take… [The child is breastfed.]
Bishakha : We can live with difficulty. What about the child? Bone-breaking cold lies ahead.
Banshidhar : I also think of that. Three more months are to pass.
Bishakha : You say four months. By that time, if my son…

| | | |
|---|---|---|
| Banshidhar | : | Why are you talking nonsense? |
| Bishakha | : | What shall I do now? Listen to me, "Let's return to Jagannathpur." |
| Banshidhar | : | Bishakha! |
| Bishakha | : | Society must have changed. (Taking a breath) Let me leave there with my son. I will come here after *Margasira* month. |
| Banshidhar | : | No, my son won't go there. |
| Bishakha | : | My son will be under these trees… what sort of dad you are! My son, in this bone-chilling cold… (to the baby) … nay…no…no…what do you say? |
| Banshidhar | : | Oh! Let me think for a while! Go there…I am making some arrangements.<br>[Bishakha takes the baby, patting its body out of discontentment. Banshidhar gets absorbed in his thoughts and looks at the bag nearby. He has shown the handle of the small axe in the bag. Questions crop up in his mind.] |
| Banshidhar's Tone | : | No…no… instead you return to your society/community, Banshidhar. |
| Banshidhar | : | I will return…I will return to my community.<br>[He quickly puts the small axe in the bag, and while running inside, the trees say.] |
| Sal | : | *manisabhāi*! |
| Banshidhar | : | I won't stay here; I can't live here. |

|  |  |
|---|---|
|  | Bishakha is right. I will return to my society. |
| Mango | : What has happened to you, *manisa bhāi*? |
| Banshidhar | : How can you understand the 'father-son relationship'? |
| Neem | : Tell, *manisa bhāi*. |
| Banshidhar | : Winter! Very cold! How can you realize this? |
| Tamarind | : Say what we can give you. Will we give fruits? |
| Banshidhar | : Branches…give me your dry branches. My little son feels cold. He trembles. His rib bones oscillate. The child will die if we don't arrange heat for his body. |
| Trees | : No…no…no… |
| Banshidhar | : Haven't I told you before that I am with fire? Tree, you give me some branches. I will help my son live comfortably, if the heat is generated in the surroundings, or else he…our Swadhin… (Crying in the dramatic pose) *ho…ho…ho…* |
| Sal | : Don't weep, *manisa bhāi*! Take… |
| Banshidhar | : Give, my brother! Give…(gratefully) Give branches, save a life, give branches, save a life.<br>[Echo in Trees' Voice: "nia…nia…nia". In the echoes, 'nia' and 'niã' are heard identically.] |
| Banshidhar | : Yes…yes…I will set a bonfire. I will set fire.<br>[Branches of one hand fall one after |

An Uninhabited Forest | 53

another from the trees. This is hinted through traditional musical sounds.]

Music : "Seeing the unending plights of living beings, how one could bear them."
Let my soul be condemned to Hell; let the world get redeemed."
[Collecting the twigs and small branches happily, while Banshidhar enters inside, the trees sing.]

Song : Take twigs, take fruits,
Save the human child.
Take roots, take flowers,
Save the human child.
[At the end of every line in the poem, a camera-clicking sound will be heard four times. That will hint that four months end. Natural changes in the trees are also marked accordingly.]
[Evening approaches. Birds have returned to their nests. Banshidhar enters disappointed. He is thoughtful in the dramatic pose.]

Mango : What happened to you, *manisa bhāi*?
Banshidhar : (Crying as if he lost his father) Everything ruined.
Neem : Your son?
Banshidhar : He is alive; my son is alive; our father died. O Tree! Our 'Father of the Nation', Mahatma Gandhi, died.
Tamarind : Was he a man?
Banshidhar : He was a great man, a great soul. If I describe his attributes, nobody can believe them. I went to my village. I

|  |  |
|---|---|
| | am returning from there only and donating my homestead land. Now I hear Gandhiji was assassinated. |
| Sal | : Who? Is he the man who assassinated him? |
| Banshidhar | : Yes, he was a man. Had he been thunderstruck or killed in the earth explosion, I would have understood. But a man like me fired the gun at him. |
| Trees | : Gun? |
| Banshidhar | : Yes gun. |
| Mango | : Do human beings keep that with them? |
| Banshidhar | : Man, himself makes a gun, Tree. (Regretfully) otherwise, how will he fire the gun secretly from a distance? One who is not within one's ambit, how can he kill? Maybe, human beings, or birds or the animals.<br>[There is agitation or stir in the birds' kingdom.] |
| Banshidhar | : (Addressing the birds) Don't worry. I am not with a gun. I won't kill anybody. I will keep my son away from those people.<br>[There is vigorous agitation in the birds' kingdom.] |
| Banshidhar | : (With folding palms all around) Birds! Don't fly away. O parrot, O myna, O cuckoo, O dove, O dung bird, O skylark! Come back. Birds, you sing songs. I will play the flute...please, come back. Don't take back your songs |

|   |   |
|---|---|
| | from the forest…come back, you all. [He brings out the flute from the bag and plays it immediately. Birds' Song.] |
| Song | : *Manisa bhāi! manisa bhāi!* Having seen you, we are afraid of. *manisa bhāi! manisa bhāi!* Having seen you, we are afraid of. [In the middle of the song, Banshidhar, playing the flute, and through eye movement, earnestly requests the birds to return. I assure you that I won't harm you.] |
| Song | : *Manisa bhāi! manisa bhāi!* You do live in our kingdom. [Birds, chirping, fly away to a safe hinterland. One hatchling dies falling near Banshidhar.] |
| Banshidhar | : (Seeing) No…no…you all come back. I will play the flute. The entire forest will be reverberated with the flute's sound. [Banshidhar plays the flute rigorously.] |
| Song | : *manisa bhāi! manisa bhāi!* We will live peacefully in the forest where no human beings reside. [The lines "We will live … where no human beings reside." Get echoed repeatedly. The birdsong gradually slows down, and the birds fly away. Banshidhar gets immersed in a dramatic pose.] |
| Sal | : Birds flew away, but what about us? |
| Mango | : How can we fly? (Trying) |

| | | |
|---|---|---|
| Neem | : | Friend, how will we fly without wings? |
| Tamarind | : | Who knows why we have not been blessed with wings? |
| Sal | : | Why, *manisa bhāi*! |
| Banshidhar | : | Had you been with wings, I would not have lived. Not even people would have lived. |
| | | [Banshidhar sits in a different pose.] |
| Sal | : | Can we ask? |
| Mango | : | Let's ask. |
| Neem | : | You ask. |
| Tamarind | : | You ask. I am terrified. |
| Neem | : | *manisa bhāi*! |
| Banshidhar | : | (Looking at) Tell me. |
| Neem | : | Are you with a gun, *manisa bhāi*!? |
| Banshidhar | : | No |
| Trees | : | (In a relaxed manner) Oh! |
| Banshidhar | : | I will stay away from guns. I live in this forest, far from the madding crowd, with my wife, Bishakha, and my son Swadhin. (Comfortably) Apart from that, how will the gun harm you, Tree? The gun may create a slight sore in your body. Can it hurt you more than that? It can't destroy you! |
| Tamarind | : | Who else can harm us, *manisa bhāi*! |
| Banshidhar | : | Other weapons. Axe, small axe, saw, etc. |
| Sal | : | Are they human beings? |
| Banshidhar | : | They sever, split, and cut into pieces… the trees, alive or dead. |
| Mango | : | Are those weapons in your bag? |

| | | |
|---|---|---|
| Banshidhar | : | (Being startled) what! |
| Mango | : | Are you with the weapons? |
| Banshidhar | : | My...my... |
| Banshidhar's tone: | | Trial by fire, Banshidhar, trial by fire! |
| Neem | : | Say, *manisa bhāi*! |
| Banshidhar's tone: | | Don't speak the truth, Banshidhar. |
| Banshidhar | : | Gandhi has taught me to speak the truth. |
| Banshidhar's tone: | | Gandhi is no more, and with him, his lessons are outdated. |
| Banshidhar | : | I am alive; my consecration has not been spent up. I will speak the truth.<br>[Echo in Tree's voice: "Say, Man! Say, Man! Say, Man!"] |
| Banshidhar | : | (Shouting) Yes, I have...yes, I have... yes, I have... (Bringing out from the bag) Here is the small axe. You all can see this.<br>[Echo in Tree's voice: "See!... See!... See!"] |
| Banshidhar | : | Hello, Brothers! This can't be called a weapon unless it is used. My leg, nails, teeth, eyes, and tongue are the weapons... (sitting tired). The world is also a weapon; soil, sky, river, mountain, and wind are weapons. (Kissing the small axe) this is also a weapon... (touching the handle). Without this, there is no weapon...you have given the handle. I will bury this under the ground. I won't sever, tear, or split anything into pieces. After that, I will say, 'I don't have any.' |

| | | |
|---|---|---|
| | | [Echo in Tree's voice: 'I don't have.' 'I don't have.' 'I don't have.'] |
| Banshidhar | : | (Getting up) ... 'I don't have.' I have no weapon, gun, fear, doubt... |
| | | [Wind's music in consolation. Tree-song] |
| Song | : | Lord, you have blessed us with a boon, |
| | | Lord, you have blessed us with a boon. |
| | | Till the time man speaks the truth, |
| | | We will sing songs and talk. |
| | | If a man lies once, |
| | | we will stop talking and be silent. |
| | | [When the tree song is continued, Banshidhar sings songs in a low voice as he presents the manifesto of human work.] |
| Song | : | Till the time man works, |
| | | You will sing and talk. |
| | | If a man sits and sleeps, |
| | | You will stop talking and be silent. |
| | | [Banshidhar, holding the small axe, moves to a place, digs the soil and buries the axe there.] |
| Song | : | I am a Man; I will speak the truth, |
| | | You will sing songs and talk. |
| | | I am a Man, I will work, |
| | | You will sing songs and talk. |
| | | [Banshidhar, while smiling, reverses the bag.] |
| Banshidhar | : | (Smiling) Empty...nothing in it. Why do you fear? |
| | | [Tree-song] |
| Song | : | No gun is in Man's bag, |

Why do we fear?
No weapon is in his hands,
Why do we fear?

Banshidhar : (Reciting rhythmically) You can see. I have no guns in my bag. Why would you fear? You can see I have no weapons in my hand, so why would you worry? Why will you be with doubts and apprehensions?

[When appropriateness, union, and firmness are maintained in the tree song, these are missing in the human song. Accordingly, through the light makeup, there is the indication of years passing.]

[Until now, some trees visible on the screen have grown old, and some are dead. Some are ruined under the soil due to old age or natural calamities, and some are standing blunted as if Belarsen stood in the Mahabharat Battle. Some new and dwarfish trees are seen in their place. The brook roars nowadays.

In line with the light arrangement focused on the back screen, the changes are perceived in the flora, and Banshidhar also grows old. He can be more than fifty now. His limbs are also feeble. There is also perceived sluggishness and sleepiness in the swiftness and skillfulness of his sensory organs. It is indicated that, for the external changes, bringing the necessary costumes from the side screen, Banshidhar changes his four kinds of acting accordingly.

Banshidhar and others' acting gradually become natural. The modernity of the stage-play is perceived in their styles, poses and acting, gestures, dress code, and dialogues. There is less presentation of lyrical poems, as seen earlier, and this lyrical style gradually disappears and is lost towards the end of the play.

When the stage lights are on, Banshidhar is seen playing the flutes and shivering. Bishakha is coughing intermittently from the inside. That is heard, and Banshidhar plays the flute and is absorbed in meditation.]

Sal : Tamarind, what has happened to the older lady?
Neem : Perhaps she will die.
Tamarind : Yes, Neem; she coughs day and night.
Sal : Why do human beings cough?
Mango : Who knows, Sal, how can we learn about human beings?

[With the increase of Bishakha's frequency and intensity of coughing, Banshidhar plays the flute intensely.]

Sal : The God of Wind has not blown out of anger- why does she tremble like this?
Mango : Perhaps someone inside her body makes her tremble.

| | | |
|---|---|---|
| Neem | : | Maybe she cleans her plights. |
| Tamarind | : | What plights will she have? |
| Neem | : | You ask! |
| Tamarind | : | You ask... *manisa bhāi*, what's your misery?<br>[Banshidhar, overlooking Tamarind, plays the flute vigorously.] |
| Sal | : | Mango, you see, someone is coming. |
| Mango | : | This is not a human child. |
| Sal | : | No...the human child does not cover the body like this. |
| Neem | : | Hey, something is in his hands. |
| Tamarind | : | It's not a weapon! |
| Sal | : | That may be the weapon. |
| Mango | : | If it is used, it will be a weapon. |
| Neem | : | Won't he use it after reaching here? |
| Mango | : | If he says, this is my weapon. |
| Sal | : | Please, hold on; we will see what's happening.<br>[Hearing the flue tuning, searching for the road, wearing a saffron dress, and dancing in the style of Lord Chaitanya, an ascetic reaches here in his frenzied or euphoric state. One can call him 'Baba Tanmayananda' appropriately. Though slightly modern, he hears the following chorus.] |
| Song | : | Brother! Have you ever seen a forest where no human beings reside?<br>[When the song ends, the ascetic is already on stage. He does not walk or run properly. That dance goes on.] |
| Babaji | : | *Aha! Aha!* (looking around) strange... |

|   |   |
|---|---|
| | How great the wonderful creation of the Almighty is here! O Lord! (To Banshidhar) Having heard the sonorous and alluring sound of the flute, I have come here, my Child! |
| Banshidhar | : (Through the flute's musical note) Who's here? |
| Babaji | : I saw a dream last night...*ha*...*ha* ... *ha*.! |
| Banshidhar | : (Through the flute's musical note) Who are you? |
| Babaji | : God told me in the dream the place in the dense forest where you would hear the flute's musical note; I would appear and stand there, too. |
| Banshidhar | : (Through the flute's musical note) You? What will it be here? |
| Babaji | : God again said, "God himself told me again that the place where the flute's musical note is played will be your holy place." |
| Banshidhar | : (He hints at the trodden path with his hand.) |
| Babaji | : (Taking a turn while going) Are you alone here, my child? |
| Banshidhar | : My wife is with me. |
| Babaji | : Amidst the forest are *ādimātā* (Shiva) and *ādipitā* (Parvati)! |
| Banshidhar | : My wife coughs. |
| Babaji | : Beautiful, very beautiful! |
| Banshidhar | : My wife? |
| Babaji | : No, my child! Married life is divinely blessed and lovely! Wife is inflicted |

| | | |
|---|---|---|
| | | with cough and cold; husband is here... |
| Banshidhar | : | (Twisting the conversation) She has a cough, cold, and asthma... |
| Babaji | : | As you have a body, you will bear disease. Your wife is diseased with asthma, but her husband is absorbed in playing the flute...Alas! My child, you understand; you understand well. |
| Banshidhar | : | What? |
| Babaji | : | Once the flute's sonorous musical note invokes God, one can be relieved from infirmity and sickness. |
| Banshidhar | : | I have not understood anything. I played the flute, but I was not happy. |
| Babaji | : | Is the cause of your suffering your wife? |
| Banshidhar | : | Now she is well. As per God's direction, she will leave for the heavenly abode. What can I do more? But my son disobeys me. |
| Babaji | : | Son? Shiva and Parvati's son Ganesh... Ganesh...! |
| Banshidhar | : | His name is Swadhina. He thinks he is entirely free... (Taking a breath) see, I talk to you a lot, but who are you? I have not called you. Where are you from? |
| Babaji | : | (Completely absorbed in) Who am I? Who am I? |
| Banshidhar | : | I don't know you, so I asked. |
| Babaji | : | I also don't know who I am. |
| Banshidhar | : | How can it be? |
| Babaji | : | I am still determining who I am, |

|   |   |
|---|---|
| | where I am from, and where I will go. I am a *Siddha purusa* who has given up society and is entirely dedicated to service to God and meditation. You touch my feet, my child! |
| Banshidhar | : Why? |
| Babaji | : Freedom (from the cycle of birth and death)! Salvation! Protection! Alas, for the protection of virtuous people... |
| Banshidhar | : Maybe, but who are you? What are you doing? |
| Babaji | : Stupid! Staying in the forest, you have forgotten the duties of the castes. |
| Banshidhar | : I might have forgotten. But what are you doing? |
| Babaji | : (Counting sacred threads he has worn) I do six rituals: the performance of a sacrifice, the act of conducting a sacrifice, learning, teaching, donating, and receiving a gift. |
| Banshidhar | : (confused) Are these activities different from each other? |
| Babaji | : Great religious rites! Religious work, divine work! Now... (extending his legs) don't delay. |
| Banshidhar | : I touch your feet when you say... (touching his feet). |
| Babaji | : Live long. I accept the service of the *Jajamana* (host or patron). |
| Banshidhar | : (Staring at him without understanding anything) |
| Babaji | : My language is advanced, Sanskrit... I agree to be your guest. |

| | | |
|---|---|---|
| Banshidhar | : | (Being startled) Who am I to accept you, my guest? (Showing the trees) ask them. |
| Babaji | : | (Looking around) Who are they? |
| Banshidhar | : | They are the trees. |
| Babaji | : | How can I ask them? |
| Banshidhar | : | If you become friends with them if they believe human beings… |
| Babaji | : | If they believe, |
| Banshidhar | : | They will believe you if you speak the truth. They will talk and share their sorrows and happiness the way they share with me… |
| Babaji | : | (Laughing at) *ha…ha…ha…* |
| Banshidhar | : | They will agree to make you, their guest. |
| Babaji | : | Directed by the Head Office, I have come here, my child? |
| Banshidhar | : | What does this mean? |
| Babaji | : | God has sent me directly… (Being overwhelmed). God said, "You will stay in the wild, dense forest where you will listen to the flute's magical sonorous sound." Beautiful, very beautiful! … (Closing his eyes) play… play … play your most alluring and hypnotizing flute's music… |
| Banshidhar | : | Do I play the flute happily? I am doing so for my wife's coughing won't be heard. |
| Babaji | : | Your wife's coughing will calm down. |
| Banshidhar | : | (With gratefulness) Please do that, Baba…she is suffering a lot. |

| | | |
|---|---|---|
| Babaji | : | Stupid! Not Baba, but Swamiji (Master). I am the master of all. |
| Banshidhar | : | Yes, that. |
| Babaji | : | Say…Swamiji! |
| Banshidhar | : | Swamiji! |
| Babaji | : | Alas! *'Jagannātha swāmi nayana pathagāmi'* (O Jagannath, Lord of the Universe, kindly be visible unto me.) … its intensity will be reduced…it's temporary…she will recover soon. |
| Banshidhar | : | (anxiously) Can she get over this illness? |
| Babaji | : | If… |
| Banshidhar | : | If? |
| Babaji | : | The degree of sins will be reduced in society. |
| Banshidhar | : | I have not committed any sin/ crime, Swamiji. |
| Babaji | : | (Smiling) *ha…ha…ha*! This world is a sinful dress. |
| Banshidhar | : | I have been away from society for a long time. |
| Babaji | : | *Ha…ha…ha*! Have you given up society? |
| Banshidhar | : | (Smiling that way) *ha…ha…ha*, yes. |
| Babaji | : | (Looking at him) Don't imitate me. Then, I will pardon you. Stupidity is forgiven. I said that a man may give up society, but society doesn't. Wherever human beings are, there is society. The forest is where the trees are. |
| Banshidhar | : | Don't talk of society, Swamiji. If you |

|   |   |
|---|---|
| | are a physician, please give me a drop of medicine (from *kamandalu*: an oblong water pot); my wife will recover from the disease. |
| Babaji | : The poor physician sells medicines, stupid! But I am not. |
| Banshidhar | : Your smile is adorable, Swamiji. |
| Babaji | : (laughing again) *ha…ha…ha*. |
| Banshidhar | : Many years ago, there was a king precisely like you in our village opera house. |
| Babaji | : I was also acting in my youth in an opera, my child. |
| Banshidhar | : Then…suddenly…Swamiji? |
| Babaji | : It's not sudden, my child. While I was engrossed in acting with a young actress… |
| Banshidhar | : Were you caught red-handed, Swamiji? |
| Babaji | : Alas! A worldly mind is caught; my child, but an ascetic, is disinterested in earthly pleasures. |
| Banshidhar | : Had this happened to you? |
| Babaji | : How won't it happen? …We were in the village Jagannathpur… |
| Banshidhar | : (Remembering)…Say…please say, Swami… |
| Babaji | : (Being overwhelmed) She was Shakuntala, I was Dushyanta! One day the older manager… our acting room… |
| Banshidhar | : Room? In our time, acting was staged in the open pandal. |

| | | |
|---|---|---|
| Babaji | : | Jay *Kalā*! If you are interested, you can do acting anywhere. |
| Banshidhar | : | After that? |
| Babaji | : | He entered our 'Acting Room'. |
| Banshidhar | : | (Retracing from memory) Yes…yes, Swamiji… |
| Babaji | : | At that time, I was discussing some mysterious tricks of acting to the heroine. The older manager, having seen us… |
| Banshidhar | : | Was he with a stick/cane, Swamiji? |
| Babaji | : | No, he was a staff himself. |
| Banshidhar | : | What does this mean? |
| Babaji | : | He was her father, an older man. |
| Banshidhar | : | Alas! |
| Babaji | : | I condemned the worldly illusion. I disowned society. I disliked the earthly life and mundane firmament I became conscious of (Chaitanya) the supreme divine light. |
| Banshidhar | : | Chaitanya (Supreme light)! Supreme light! |
| Babaji | : | What happened? |
| Banshidhar | : | No, no…at our time, the boys were acting the heroine's role. I thought the heroine's name might be Chaitanya. |
| Babaji | : | (Being overwhelmed) At our time, the boys also took part in the women's roles. |
| Banshidhar | : | After that? |
| Babaji | : | I developed a sense of detachment. |
| Banshidhar | : | Oh, you became an ascetic. |

| | | |
|---|---|---|
| Babaji | : | (Being confused) Staring at...how did you know I became an ascetic? |
| Banshidhar | : | From your get-up |
| Babaji | : | Then, I agree to be your guest...the unsociable... |
| Banshidhar | : | My name is Banshidhar. |
| Babaji | : | (Recollecting) Banshidhar, Banshidhar... yes, as you play the flute, your name must be Banshidhar...(pretending) What will you gain from the names? We are all the children of God, no matter what our names may be. All of us must cross the world Baitarini River to reach *Amaradhāma* (heaven/eternal abode) ...alas! Baitarini, Baitarini...marching ahead on Baitarini. |
| Banshidhar | : | No Baitarini is here but a fountain, Swamiji. |
| Babaji | : | Let your *manskāmanā* (wishes/desires) be fulfilled, my child! |
| Banshidhar | : | What are my wishes...? |
| Babaji | : | It is the host's responsibility to show the sources of water for bathing and purification of the body. |
| Banshidhar | : | (Guessing) You want to take a bath! |
| Babaji | : | In the chilling cold, taking a bath is not unavoidable, my child! Only purification is not faulty. |
| Banshidhar | : | I understood, Swamiji. I have cleaned the bank of the brook. |
| Babaji | : | Alas! You are devoted to your service. Then I will return. |
| Banshidhar | : | Will you come? Here? |

| | | |
|---|---|---|
| Babaji | : | After purification of my body, whatever you offer to your guest… |
| Banshidhar | : | What can I offer to you, Swamiji? We live on fruits. I last saw rice many years ago. |
| Babaji | : | No need to worry…sweet fruits can be relished. |
| Banshidhar | : | (Looking at the trees) … if they offer… |
| Babaji | : | Who will give? |
| Banshidhar | : | Trees. Sometimes, they deny offering fruits. |
| Babaji | : | *ha…ha…ha*! |
| Babaji | : | (Not believing) I have come here following Head Office's Order…you touch my feet… |
| Banshidhar | : | You return from the bank of the fountain. |
| Babaji | : | Then you will touch my feet again… the scriptures say, the religion says this. |
| Banshidhar | : | When you say … (He touches.) |
| Babaji | : | Beautiful! Very beautiful! O Lord, Supreme Soul, the Great… [Reciting an unwanted verse of Sanskrit unnecessarily and modifying it, Babaji leaves the spot.] |
| Neem | : | *manisa bhāi*! |
| Banshidhar | : | Yes |
| Tamarind | : | He is also a human being. |
| Banshidhar | : | Yes, he is but an ascetic. |
| Mango | : | Can he speak the truth? |
| Banshidhar | : | No |
| Sal | : | Does he work? |

## An Uninhabited Forest | 71

| | | |
|---|---|---|
| Banshidhar | : | Yes, he does but *bābāgiri* (ascetic works/ ritual rites). |
| Tamarind | : | What kind of ascetic work does he do? |
| Banshidhar | : | Yajana…(remembering) jajana… purification…I am forgetting another concept. |
| Neem | : | He lives alone. |
| Banshidhar | : | He depends upon God only. [Tree-smile] |
| Trees | : | *Hi…hi…hi…hi…* |
| Banshidhar | : | (Smiling) *Hi…hi…hi…hi…* |
| Sal | : | Buddy, why does a man touch another's feet? |
| Mango | : | How will we know? It does not happen to us. |
| Neem | : | You can ask! |
| Tamarind | : | *manisa bhāi*! Why did you touch the feet of an ascetic? |
| Banshidhar | : | As I did not touch the feet of the white sepoy, my wife Lalita died. I had to leave my society; This local Babaji (ascetic) forced me to touch his feet. |
| Trees | : | Why? [Echo in the trees' voice: "Why… why…why…why"] |
| Banshidhar | : | Common people, through these ascetics reach the Supreme Being, Tree. |
| Trees | : | Why? Why? [There is an echo heard.] |
| Banshidhar's tone: | | You were afraid of him. He threatened you. |
| Banshidhar | : | (fearfully) what! |

| | |
|---|---|
| Banshidhar's tone : | Religion...scriptures...Freedom... Salvation...Infirmity/old age...sin... these threatened you. |
| Banshidhar : | (Shouting) No! |
| | [Tree-song] |
| Song : | Religion threatens you,<br>Scriptures threaten you,<br>If you live by working,<br>Who can threaten you?<br>The weapons threaten you as much as the scriptures,<br>If you consider your work as religion, we will talk to you.<br>[The last line of Tree-song gets diffused in the air gradually. After that, Banshidhar's son Swadhin comes out. He resembles Banshidhar. He is a twenty-four-year-old young man. He has an unshaved beard and hair uncaringly. Looking at him, Banshidhar is irritated. Swadhin also reciprocates his look.] |
| Banshidhar : | (Taking a turn) Very bad! |
| Swadhin : | (Entering inside) What bad! (He has gone inside.)<br>[Banshidhar brings out the flute. He is playing the flute so Swadhin can clean his face. He takes a pose to play the flute. Before he starts, Swadhin has come out.] |
| Swadhin : | (Having seen him) *hun*! |
| Banshidhar : | (Putting the flute in its place) *hun*!<br>[At one time, Swadhin moves outside, |

and Banshidhar enters inside. The father-son relationship becomes so bitter that they are not ready to understand or accept each other. When the lights are off for a moment, and again immediately, it is seen that Swadhin has come from outside. Banshidhar has come from inside.]

Banshidhar : Where have you gone?
Swadhin : I have gone.
Banshidhar : Where have you been for the last two days?
Swadhin : I have been to somewhere (While entering inside)
Banshidhar : Are you going inside?
Swadhin : Inside! A house does have an inside and an outside; what's here inside and outside in the jungle?
Banshidhar : Go and see how your mother's health is.
Swadhin : I have seen. (standing) As I can't see my mother's condition, I don't stay here for a moment. I had gone somewhere from here.
Banshidhar : (with apprehension) Where have you gone for long?
Swadhin : Why do you ask me?
Banshidhar : (with apprehension) Have you visited the Society?
Swadhin : Does it matter to you whether I visited or not?
Banshidhar : Can't I ask you whether you went or not?

| | | |
|---|---|---|
| Swadhin | : | How can I stay here? |
| Banshidhar | : | Why can you? Your mother is on her deathbed, but her son is telling...*hun*? |
| Swadhin | : | Who has instructed you to allow my mom to rest under the trees? |
| Banshidhar | : | Otherwise? |
| Swadhin | : | Indeed, I have been far away from home. But what about you? You stayed at your home during your childhood! You can build a house like that! Hot summer, heavy rainfall, chilled winter - if anyone stays outside like this... |
| Banshidhar | : | Hello, what is outside? What is outside? |
| Swadhin | : | (showing inside) That's outside... (Stamping his feet) this is outside... (Going to Banshidhar) this is outside... (Going to another place) this...this is outside... (stamping the feet) ... this one... |
| | | [The small axe is buried there. While stamping the feet, Swadhin stops there.] |
| Banshidhar | : | (Being terrified) What happened? |
| Swadhin | : | (Stamping his feet) The land seems soft and soggy here. |
| Banshidhar | : | What? |
| Swadhin | : | The soil seems to be boggy here. It has no strength. Different sound comes out here. |
| | | [He makes a comparative study of that place and a nearby place.] |
| Swadhin | : | Soil is dug here. Who came here? |

An Uninhabited Forest | 75

[He said he sits there and removes grass on its bed. Banshidhar looked at Swadhin as if he had buried his sin there. When Swadhin extracts soil from there with his hands, Banshidhar runs there with an extraordinary force and drags Swadhin. Swadhin falls at a distance and gets injured. But he is startled at Banshidhar's such behaviour.]

| | | |
|---|---|---|
| Swadhin | : | (With surprise) Papa! |
| Banshidhar | : | Are you digging home? |
| Swadhin | : | Home? |
| Banshidhar | : | Yes, this is home… (Stamping feet and normalizing the soil) this is home… that is also home. That is also…the entire forest is our home, do you understand? You are born here. |
| Swadhin | : | Was I born on my own? If someone had asked me, I would not have come to such a house. |
| Banshidhar | : | Swadhin! |
| Swadhin | : | Who is Swadhin? You have explained to me what Swadhin means. It means 'Nobody is above me.' Nobody will instruct me. |
| Banshidhar | : | Who instructs you? |
| Swadhin | : | Tiger, Bear, Snake, Mosquito, Gadfly |
| Banshidhar | : | (Stares at him without reply) |
| Swadhin | : | (Changing the tone) Listening to me, let's return to the society. |
| Banshidhar | : | You will also find tigers, bears, etc. there….but they are not visible to the |

|  |  |
|---|---|
| | naked eye. Yes, I won't be there to instruct or order you. |
| Swadhin | : I am not saying that… (taking a breath); otherwise, build a house here so that all of us will stay happily. |
| Banshidhar | : Are you unhappy? |
| Swadhin | : O dad, why don't you understand? |
| Banshidhar | : Don't make me understand? I am your father. Hey, what have I not given you? |
| Swadhin | : (Out of anger) House…you have not given me a house. No roof is built for me. |
| Banshidhar | : How will we build a house? Do we need wood or not? Tell me. |
| Swadhin | : You know this. |
| Banshidhar | : We need big logs. Where will we get logs? |
| Swadhin | : (confused) Where will we get the logs? What does this mean? |
| Banshidhar | : Yes, where will we get logs? |
| Swadhin | : (Sarcastically) Where will we get… wood? One will laugh at us; where will we get wood if my mother's dead body is before us? (Easily) Wood comes from the forest. |
| Banshidhar | : It does not come; it is brought; it is split into pieces, severed, and torn. Forest does not give us wood as the sky showers. The people snatch away the calves while milking the cow. |
| Swadhin | : Well, we will do that. What we won't get will be forcefully brought, cut and torn. |

## An Uninhabited Forest | 77

| | | |
|---|---|---|
| Banshidhar | : | *Hun* (a sound of defiance) |
| Swadhin | : | Bring a small axe, cut down the trees, and build the house for us. |
| Banshidhar | : | Before that, you chop me into pieces… |
| Swadhin | : | (Silent) |
| Banshidhar | : | Why do you stand? Chop me into pieces. No, no, all mistakes are mine. |
| Swadhin | : | Otherwise, how I am wrong!<br>[Having heard the father-son quarrel, Bishakha, who has asthma, comes moaning. Before she falls to the ground, Swadhin holds her fall halfway.] |
| Swadhin | : | Staying under the trees and eating fruits, how many days can one live? |
| Bishakha | : | Swa…dhi…na…. Swa…dhi…na…<br>[The number of times Bishakha starts to intervene to sort out the issue between father and son, she gets defeated by her asthma. She only emits a hissing sound like a snake.] |
| Swadhin | : | Can you see my mother's condition? You said, "The physician can set right the disease and prescribe medicine; I am calling him now." |
| Bishakha | : | (Shaking her hand) No…no… |
| Swadhin | : | You don't support my father; otherwise, you will die. What's that river? I have forgotten its name. Here, you won't get a drop of *Gangajal*. |
| Bishakha | : | (Touching Swadhin's chin) When you are here with me…I have everything. |
| Swadhin | : | For breakfast in the morning, we use |

|  |  |
|---|---|
|  | mango, jackfruit, gourd, and pumpkin. For lunch in the afternoon- pumpkin, gourd, jackfruit and mango. For dinner at night- jackfruit, pumpkin, mango, and gourd. We have the same fruits and vegetables, whether happy, unhappy, or diseased. *Hun*! (a sound of defiance) |
| Banshidhar | : Yes, yes...taking those mango, jackfruit, gourd, and pumpkin, you are grown up. You are strong and energetic now. |
| Swadhin | : (Out of irritation) What I gained from those was okay. I don't need them now. If I were more energetic, the tigers and bears would hide themselves, having seen me. Because of this strength, the chilling cold of winter, the autumn dews, the scorching rays of summer, and raindrops won't touch me. (Nearing his mother) Mom, you help him understand...we must cut down some trees and build one house for us. |
| Banshidhar | : How will she help me understand? Listen to me; I am determined not to cut down the trees and won't allow others to do so. These are not fruit-bearing trees. These trees are equivalent to gold for me. |
| Swadhin | : I have never seen Gold here... (Picking up a dry fruit from the ground) ...is this gold? |
| Banshidhar | : Yes, that's gold... |

| | | |
|---|---|---|
| Swadhin | : | (Allowing his father to hold that fruit) Then keep it, lick, and stay here in your gold forest... (while going) ... you can also be here...if you become breathless because of asthma, you will lick the gold...*hun*. |
| | | [While Swadhin kicks the dried fruits on the ground, he stumbles and is about to fall; Banshidhar and Bishakha run to hold him, but he does not fall and leaves. Bishakha becomes breathless for her running. Banshidhar allows her to sit on a rock. They look at each other. A rehearsal of the classical 'Shree' musical mode is heard slowly. Because of a winter evening, Bishakha shivers in cold and pain.] |
| Neem | : | Mango, *manisa bhāi* gets annoyed with his grown-up son. |
| Mango | : | Why do the human beings get annoyed? |
| Neem | : | How will we know? |
| Tamarind | : | Can you be angry? |
| Neem | : | I? Okay, let me try. [Neem Tree slightly tilts or shakes her body.] |
| Sal | : | You are dancing, Neem? You are not angry. |
| Neem | : | You tell me how to be angry. |
| Mango | : | Can we ask it to *manisaa bhāi*? |
| Sal | : | If he gets angry at us? |
| Mango | : | If he gets angry at us, I will drop some fruit! How come a mango in winter? |

| | | |
|---|---|---|
| Neem | : | Call him. |
| Mango | : | (Calling) *manisaa bhāi*! |
| Banshidhar | : | (Out of anger) what? |
| | | [A mango dropped near him.] |
| Banshidhar | : | (Happily) A mango in winter! Bishakha, you see… |
| | | [Bishakha, glad, tried to praise God's grace but failed. At last, the sound 'he…he…' comes from her throat.] |
| Bishakha | : | (With folding palms) O Maa Hingulai, O Maa Jagulai, O Maa Bais, O Maa Baras, hey Maa, hey Maa, hey Maa… |
| | | [Later, only hissing sounds came out of her.] |
| Banshidhar | : | Bishakha…Bishakha… |
| Bishakha | : | (Unsteadily) Tell me… |
| Banshidhar | : | Are you not going to leave me permanently? |
| Bishakha | : | (Nodding her head, she shakes her hands.) |
| Banshidhar | : | I have one closely linked to me… |
| Bishakha | : | (She shows the road Swadhin has already marched on.) |
| Banshidhar | : | He doesn't listen to me. We can't share our feelings. He is advanced, like a city person. He says, cut down the trees, build a house, and be socialized… will I cut down these trees? They have given him life. they are our neighbours… (Showing the trees) this is Rama Kaka, this is Shama Bhai, my *Gelhi* (pampered daughter) is here… Nani…and you at that, how it looks |

An Uninhabited Forest | 81

at us...a stupid fellow. My son was happy in their company.
[The innocent and enticing smile of a five to six-year-old son is heard, and Banshidhar and Bishakha are standing in the dim light. The boy's sound is heard from a tree's side.]

| | | |
|---|---|---|
| Banshidhar | : | Swadhin! |
| Boy | : | Papa...you search me... |
| Banshidhar | : | Swadhin, where are you now? |
| Boy | : | (Imitating the tiger's roaring) Here...here... |
| Banshidhar | : | Where? |
| Boy | : | Here, behind Rama Kaka... |
| Banshidhar | : | I am giving you... (Looking at the backside of Sal Tree) Hey, where are you hiding? |
| Boy | : | Search for me...I am here, at Shama Bhai's side... |
| Banshidhar | : | I know they will spoil you. |

[It is true that when they address trees like Rama Kaka and Shama Bhai, there is no perceived Generation Gap.]

| | | |
|---|---|---|
| Banshidhar | : | Come... |
| Boy | : | Say that you will bring a new towel for me... |
| Banshidhar | : | Yes, I will bring it from Haripur *Hāt*. Come on... |
| Boy | : | Nani says to wait. She will give me mangoes. |
| Banshidhar | : | I am looking at you, and your Nani too. |

[The boy, coming from the tree side,

|  |  |  |
|---|---|---|
|  |  | enters inside. He wears a towel only. While going...] |
| Banshidhar | : | O get hold of him...get hold of him...I have got hold of him now.<br>[The light has come to the zone where Banshidhar and Bishakha stand.] |
| Banshidhar | : | Now he is beyond my control...I can't understand him. I caught hold of him while hiding behind the trees, but will he hide in the society or the city? (Suddenly) won't you leave me, Bishakha? Won't you hide yourself like the stars?<br>[Banshidhar starts crying. Bishakha is crying. Trees talk.] |
| Neem | : | Trees give birth to trees... |
| Tamarind | : | Birds give birth to birds... |
| Sal | : | Animals give birth to animals... |
| Mango | : | What do the human beings give birth to? |
| Banshidhar | : | (cajoling with apprehension) Hey! (To Bishakha, slowly) what do human beings reproduce? (Shaking her body) what are the offspring of human beings? |
| Bishakha | : | (Shaking her head) I don't know. (Shaking her hands) I don't know. |
| Song | : | "What the human children become is not known to them,<br>Say what the human beings understand is not known to God."<br>[When the last line, after the echo, gets reduced in intensity, Banshidhar shouts.] |

| | | |
|---|---|---|
| Banshidhar | : | Who knows what they will become, who knows what they will be! Whatever it may be, Bishakha, I have no fear when you are with me. |
| Bishakha | : | (shaking her head and hands) I…and I… |
| Banshidhar | : | No…no…hear, beneath the bald hill, there are the Arka shrubs/ plants. We will go there. You will recover from your illness if you drink a drop of Arka (Giant milkweed) milk. You will work again. If you don't work, they won't give you fruits. What will you eat? Come on, please come… |

[After Bishakha starts walking, shouldering on Banshidhar in one direction (From right to left of the audience), the trees move slowly in the opposite direction (From left to right).]

[Through the movement of different lights, there is the hint that some years have passed. A dirty environment is indicated through a dark brown, lifeless colour. Loneliness is perceived everywhere. The trees shown through the back screen are almost invisible. A portion of the grey and empty sky is visible.]

[An infant song is heard by a boy or girl nearby. A mouth organ is also played in that voice/tone.]

| | |
|---|---|
| Infant-song | : Twinkle, twinkle, little star, How I wonder what you are, Up above the world so high, Like a diamond in the sky. [When the nursery rhyme is continued in a low voice, Babaji enters. Hair and beard are slightly whitened. He looks around as if he lost his path. Putting his fingers on his nostrils, he is determined to move in one direction; he comes back again, having covered a small distance.] |
| Babaji | : Have you lost your path in the forest? Banshidhar, on this side…no, not on this side…not at all…who said on this side? Yes, on this side…but many trees were on this side, where are they? (Looking above) There is no sunlight! Nowadays, he takes leave for twenty days a month… [Some verses of *Vishnu Sahasranāma* are wrongly recited.] |
| Verses | : *hiranyaka garbha bhūgarbha madhav he madhusūdan…* (Being afraid of) O Madhav, O Madhusudan…O…O… [The Boy's nursery rhyme is heard.] |
| Babaji | : Who? Who is roaring? Who is there? [The nursery rhyme is stopped.] |
| Babaji | : Come to the front…(whimsically) One uses English! [Now Swadhin produces an animal's loud call: *"huke ho", "huke ho"* (Like a |

## An Uninhabited Forest | 85

|                    |   |                                                                                                                                                                                                                                                                                                 |
|--------------------|---|-------------------------------------------------------------------------------------------------------------------------------------------------------------------------------------------------------------------------------------------------------------------------------------------------|
|                    |   | jackal's howling). Babaji listens to the sound.]                                                                                                                                                                                                                                                |
| Babaji             | : | (Welcoming) It's nearby…(Happily) it is found, after many years, there is a road in the forest… (Out of anger) It is not the jackal! Who's there? (Courageously) Who's there? *huke ho*?                                                                                                        |
| Swadhin's tone     | : | *huke ho, huke ho*!                                                                                                                                                                                                                                                                              |
| Babaji             | : | *huke ho, huke ho*!                                                                                                                                                                                                                                                                              |
| Babaji             | : | (Hearing) It may not be jackal… (happily) Man is found, after many years in the forest…I will trace the road soon…(imitating) *huke ho, huke ho*!                                                                                                                                                |
|                    |   | [Babaji says, "*huke ho, huke ho*", standing in one direction. Without getting any reply, standing like a jackal, when Babaji says "*huke ho, huke ho*" again in another direction, Swadhin, coming behind him, plays mouth organ at his nape.]                                                 |
| Swadhin            | : | Say again, once more.                                                                                                                                                                                                                                                                           |
| Babaji             | : | What will I say, my child? (He gets up.)                                                                                                                                                                                                                                                        |
| Swadhin            | : | Don't move an inch. Hands up… (Babaji raises his hands.) What's with you?                                                                                                                                                                                                                        |
| Babaji             | : | (Gesticulating) I don't have anything except the *kamandalu* (Oblong brass water pot), my child.                                                                                                                                                                                                 |
| Swadhin            | : | What's there inside?                                                                                                                                                                                                                                                                            |
| Babaji             | : | Empty…full of emptiness.                                                                                                                                                                                                                                                                        |
| Swadhin            | : | Emptiness? Was that a code word?                                                                                                                                                                                                                                                                |

| | | |
|---|---|---|
| Babaji | : | My child? |
| Swadhin | : | Is there any weapon inside? |
| Babaji | : | Weapon? How will it help me? |
| Swadhin | : | Everybody needs weapons. |
| Babaji | : | (Keeping his mouth ajar) My speech is my weapon, my child. |
| Swadhin | : | Very clever... (He reverses the *kamandalu* and has found nothing.) Nothing is inside. |
| Babaji | : | Unholy! I read *dharma* with that *kamandalu*, my child. |
| Swadhin | : | (Out of aversion) *Dharma*! |
| Babaji | : | What's there at my nape? It looks like a machine. |
| Swadhin | : | Weapon...pistol...I will remove your skull. |
| Babaji | : | (out of fear) what... |
| Swadhin | : | Say... *huke ho, huke ho*... |
| Babaji | : | (Trembling in fear) *huke ho, huke ho, huke ho, huke ho*... |
| Swadhin | : | Stand up... (Babaji stands up trembling.) Now you say who you are. |
| Babaji | : | *siddha purusa*. |
| Swadhin | : | Where are you from? Why do you loiter here? |
| Babaji | : | I went to wash off my body. Remove that pistol. Otherwise, I will have to go again.<br>[Swadhin puts the mouth organ secretly in his pocket.] |
| Swadhin | : | After that? |
| Babaji | : | I didn't find the source of water. The |

## An Uninhabited Forest | 87

| | | |
|---|---|---|
| | | brook is dry. I have not cleaned. Then, I am searching for a way to return. |
| Swadhin | : | How many days had it been? |
| Babaji | : | I can't count. I have been searching for the path for many years. Where is the path? |
| Swadhin | : | Where will you go? |
| Babaji | : | I don't know. If God instructs… |
| Swadhin | : | Don't try to deceive me. In which department are you working- Police, C.I.D., C.B.I., or I.S.I.? |
| Babaji | : | I don't have any department, my child. I am an ascetic. Touch my feet. |
| Swadhin | : | Why will I touch your feet? |
| Babaji | : | Freedom! Salvation! Protection…the protection of the good or virtuous people… |
| Swadhin | : | I don't believe in those nonsense words. Can you give me roti? Roti? |
| Babaji | : | I don't eat roti, my child. I take only fruit and water. |
| Swadhin | : | We will eat. We are three in number. |
| Babaji | : | (Being hopeful) Is any human habitant here, my child? |
| Swadhin | : | No |
| Babaji | : | For whom are you asking for roti? Roti is not meant for the tigers or the bears… |
| Swadhin | : | "Don't ask. Answer me what you are being asked." The first rule of our party. |
| Babaji | : | Your party? Which party are you in? |
| Swadhin | : | Don't ask. If Guruji knows, you will be flogged. |

| | | |
|---|---|---|
| Babaji | : | Guruji? |
| Swadhin | : | Are you asking again? |
| Babaji | : | I don't belong to your party. I am *Siddha purusa*; my job is to ask others. |
| Swadhin | : | (Looking around cautiously) "Guruji is our Netaji; he watches everything." This is our second rule. |
| Babaji | : | (Teasing) What's your third rule, my dear? |
| Swadhin | : | (Saying like a machine) "What Guruji does is right." Okay. |
| Babaji | : | This is the Eleventh Incarnation! Is he God? |
| Swadhin | : | He is God for us. His *Baikunthapur* (i.e., our headquarters) is nearby. And hear… |
| Babaji | : | I am well known as Swamiji, my child. [It is hinted that the characters gradually become rude after entering the normal stage.] |
| Swadhin | : | I don't need to know. Guruji wants to see if you command the trees to bear rotis by *mantra tantra*. (any sacred formula or the magical spell). |
| Babaji | : | Tree? (thinking of himself) Yes, yes… Yes, I can… (looking around), but my child! No trees are seen here. |
| Swadhin | : | Trees are at some place. I will show you. (Staying for a while) Don't you joke at me? |
| Babaji | : | If I come across the trees, I can extract rotis from the trees by sacred formulae…you will see the trees |

## An Uninhabited Forest | 89

|          |   |                                                                                                                             |
|----------|---|-----------------------------------------------------------------------------------------------------------------------------|
|          |   | bearing big rounded rotis. You will believe that Lord (remembering) Madhav, Madhusudan, has hung the fresh rotis in the tree branches. But my Child (showing displeasure), how many rotis do you need? |
| Swadhin  | : | Two…two…four…all together, apart from you, we need eight. What about you? |
| Babaji   | : | I only take fruits and water. |
| Swadhin  | : | Then, for today, we need only eight. |
| Babaji   | : | Can't you adjust with fruits? |
| Swadhin  | : | Guruji won't eat fruits. I may adjust, but Guruji… |
| Babaji   | : | Sweet and delicious fruits are the prasad to the Gods and Goddesses, my child. |
| Swadhin  | : | Guruji is not God but a man. He is with diabetes. |
| Babaji   | : | (Not understanding) Beautiful! Very beautiful!! |
| Swadhin  | : | (Stepping forward) What is beautiful? |
| Babaji   | : | (withdrawing)…taking roti as the meals |
| Swadhin  | : | "What Guruji does is right." |
| Babaji   | : | I also agree with him. |
| Swadhin  | : | Hear, there is no food in the storeroom. A supply should reach us from the society but couldn't. Can you generate eight rotis for us? |
| Babaji   | : | (with pretension) Eight? (Looking at Swadhin) I have not attended the complete power of a *Siddha purusa*, |

|  |  |
|---|---|
| | my child. (Remembering God) *O Mahimāmaya Paramapurusa*! I have limited knowledge. |
| Swadhin | : What had I to lose? |
| Babaji | : I can generate two rotis from each tree. So, I need four trees. Where are the trees? |
| Swadhin | : I have told you to show. |
| Babaji | : At one place. I had a dream, my child. God said, "The place where Sal, Mango, Neem, and Tamarind trees are found together, there resides God, the Almighty." By my sacred formula, each tree will bear two rotis only… (looking at Swadhin) big rounded fresh rotis! |
| Swadhin | : Yes, such a place is inside the jungle. I know. |
| Babaji | : Nice! Very nice!! Again, I dreamed the magical flute sound would be heard intermittently amidst the trees. That is *Mohan Banśi*. |
| Swadhin | : Yes, I will show you exactly that place. |
| Babaji | : God's dream will be in vain. Alas! The forest is your Guru; what's your name? Yes, Uddhav…why are you asking me a lot? |
| Swadhin | : I still doubt. |
| Babaji | : Doubt? *Ha…ha…ha…*! We can get rotis by faith only. |
| Swadhin | : Truly? |
| Babaji | : Delay is dangerous. Lead me to that divine place immediately, my child. |

| | | |
|---|---|---|
| Swadhin | : | When you say, please come. |
| Babaji | : | I don't go like this, my child. |
| Swadhin | : | If you want, I will shoulder you. |
| Babaji | : | Touching my body is prohibited. Touching my feet is a must. |
| Swadhin | : | Our party's manifesto has declared that one should not touch another's feet, Babaji. |
| Babaji | : | (Trembling in fear) Stupid! Am I an ordinary man? |
| Swadhin | : | (slightly fearful) then? |
| Babaji | : | I am a *siddha purusa*, an ascetic Swamiji. |
| Swadhin | : | Swamiji? |
| Babaji | : | (Speaking softly) Alas! (extending his feet) Clear doubts from your mind, man. Touching my feet means touching the half heaven. |
| Swadhin | : | Guruji says, "We are people; we need earth only, and we don't need heaven. Swamiji!" |
| Babaji | : | (with a hand posture) You need the rotis.<br>[Swadhin is forced to touch Babaji's feet.] |
| Babaji | : | You touch my feet.<br>[He has blessed Swadhin.] |
| Babaji | : | Live long, you will be successful in your party's work. March ahead… let's walk… |
| Swadhin | : | Let's go, Swami.<br>[While Swadhin is ready to walk first and Babaji next, the nursery rhyme is again heard.] |

| | | |
|---|---|---|
| Nursery Rhyme | : | Twinkle, twinkle, little star |
| | | How I wonder what you are |
| | | Up above the world so high |
| | | Like a diamond in the sky. |
| | | [Swadhin, getting afraid of, stops there.] |
| Babaji | : | Who sings twinkle, twinkle? |
| Swadhin | : | *en*! (An expression of denial.) |
| | | [Swadhin looks at the direction of the source of the song.] |
| Babaji | : | Let's move, my child! |
| Swadhin | : | Yes, we will go. |
| Babaji | : | (Stepping ahead) 'Twinkle, twinkle, little star…how I wonder what you are.' (Swadhin hears this.) |
| Swadhin | : | Please stop! |
| Babaji | : | You won't say who is singing; you deny me to sing; you won't go ahead; you will deny me to go. |
| Swadhin | : | Shut up, Swamiji! |
| Babaji | : | (Saying while walking) You won't wash off yourself; clean space won't leave me… (taking a breath) I ask you who is singing. |
| Swadhin | : | Muna…Muna |
| Babaji | : | Muna, why are you singing here? |
| Swadhin | : | He must be remembering his home. |
| Babaji | : | Who is he? Where is his house? Why is he here, and what does he do here? |
| Swadhin | : | (mechanically) "Don't ask me anything; you answer what you are asked." I have been told not to reply. |
| Babaji | : | Say who has denied you. I will deny |

## An Uninhabited Forest | 93

|  |  |  |
|---|---|---|
|  |  | him by the *mantra* (sacred formula) who has denied you. |
| Swadhin | : | Guruji |
| Nursery Rhyme | : | Twinkle, twinkle, little star… |
| Swadhin | : | (Facing that side) *huke ho, huke ho*! |
| Babaji | : | What's this again? Twinkle, *Huke*. Am I here on this earth? Feel my pulse rate and say whether I am alive. |
| Swadhin | : | Up till now, you have been alive. |
| Babaji | : | (Being afraid of) Up till now, I have been alive. What does this mean? What after this? [Babaji, in the name of God with folding palms, chants some portions of *Visnusahasra Nāma* and some portion of *Hanumān Caliśā*, wrongly, in the voice of a popular film song.] |
| Babaji | : | *nirākāra nirādhāra nirābhāsa nirāśraya mahāvīra vikram bajarangi kumati nibāra sumati ke sangi he madhusūdan mādhava he…* |
| Swadhin | : | Stop it. (Babaji opens his eyes) Your Madhav (God) won't know our human activities. |
| Babaji | : | Who else knows… |
| Swadhin | : | The person who frames the rules is our Guruji himself. |
| Babaji | : | What will happen? |
| Swadhin | : | You may be punished. |
| Babaji | : | Your Guruji … to me death? (Trying to laugh at uselessly) *ha…ha…ha…he… he…he…* |
| Swadhin | : | "What Guruji does is right." |

| | | |
|---|---|---|
| Babaji | : | Then, he will decide not to kill me because I can't die. I am on the path of righteousness. In my dream, God has ordered me to complete the work before my death. |
| Swadhin | : | Guruji won't die. He will only die after he completes the party's work. |
| Babaji | : | (sarcastically) Who is that Guruji, and what's his work? |
| Nursery Rhyme | : | Twinkle, twinkle, little star... |
| Babaji | : | (Unnecessarily shouting) Stop your twinkle rhyme... |
| Swadhin | : | (answering back) *huke ho, huke ho!* |
| Babaji | : | Stop your *huke ho, huke ho!* Say your Guruji's name, or I won't instruct the trees to bear rotis. |
| Swadhin | : | Guruji comes. |

[Swadhin stands in front of Babaji. They look at him. Putting his hands on the shoulder of a boy named Muna or a girl named Muni Guruji, who seems to be above eighty, comes immediately. He holds a crutch in his hands. He is weak due to illness. His beard and hair on his head are entirely grey. His dress means a half-blue suit and a full, long red sweater. The eyes are shining from behind the goggles. Discussion is to the point, and the party's constitutional rules are like the journalists' press meet announcements.

The boy or the girl's age will be

An Uninhabited Forest | 95

approximately nine. She wears a uniform from the Women's Convent School. There is no fickle-mindedness or lyrical flow in conversation. In the acting, dryness and lifelessness are marked freshly consecrated or newly trained. The acting sans all human sensibility indicates that he is, as if, the only one to survive after the nuclear explosion or the prescribed words of doomsday/ apocalyptic war as enshrined in the Malika will happen shortly before this man. It is clear from his mouth that "I am the end." He behaves like a robot, though not at all a machine. With the arrival of these two characters, the environment seems dry, lifeless, brownish, and sterile. From Banshidhar to Muna or Muni is an endless document of degeneration.]

| | | |
|---|---|---|
| Guruji | : | 1947 |
| Swadhin | : | Guruji! |
| Guruji | : | Give me roti. |
| Muna/Muni | : | Guruji asks for roti, 1947. [Hint: Only Muna is written after this.] |
| Guruji | : | I am not begging for, 1984. Begging is prohibited. 'Roti' is my right. |
| Swadhin | : | There is no more roti, Guruji. |
| Guruji | : | How come it finished? I did not have. |
| Swadhin | : | Now we don't have rotis, Guruji. |
| Guruji | : | Have you finished all? |
| Swadhin | : | No, I have also not eaten. The supply |

|  |  |
|---|---|
|  | from the headquarters has yet to arrive. |
| Guruji | : Whose responsibility was to deliver the supply? |
| Swadhin | : 1965 and 1971 |
| Guruji | : (as if releasing acid breath) Okay… |
| Swadhin | : We don't have atta and potatoes in our stock. |
| Guruji | : The Police seized. |
| Swadhin | : Impossible. |
| Guruji | : Have you contacted through wireless? |
| Swadhin | : There is no signal, Guruji. |
| Guruji | : Oh, I see! Getting that opportunity, you were running away. |
| Swadhin | : (Fearfully) no…no… |
| Guruji | : I have told you that you will be here forever, once you are in. Then all your doors are closed. |
| Swadhin | : I was not running away, Guruji. |
| Guruji | : It's the blind lane. Guruji sits on one of its ends while the other is closed. |
| Swadhin | : I went to the party's work to collect the rotis. |
| Guruji | : Where is roti? (Greedily) I need roti now. |
| Swadhin | : This Swami says he will help the trees bear rotis. |
| Muna | : How can rotis be born by the trees? |
| Guruji | : Who is he? |
| Babaji | : I am a *siddha purusa*. Touch my feet, my child! |
| Swadhin | : (Denying) What do you say, Swamiji? |
| Guruji | : Will I touch your feet? |

| | | |
|---|---|---|
| Swadhin | : | No...no...Guruji, the Swamiji, inadvertently said so. |
| Babaji | : | No, my child! I have said this knowingly- for his freedom, salvation, and protection. |
| Guruji | : | What's your number? |
| Babaji | : | There is no number of *anādi ananta*. |
| Guruji | : | Well, what's your number? |
| Babaji | : | You may assume 'Dharma'. You will touch my feet now. |
| Guruji | : | The party has denied- you won't touch anybody's feet. |
| Babaji | : | One who will provide you food...I mean to say you won't touch that person's feet who will give you roti. |
| Guruji | : | Will you have roti? |
| Babaji | : | I am *siddha purusa*. What I eat is green and fresh. |
| Muna | : | You eat green and fresh. |
| Babaji | : | Yes, my child, I only eat green and fresh. |
| Guruji | : | Where will the rotis be born or made, 1947? |
| Swadhin | : | I have seen that spot. I will lead you all; it is nearby. |
| Muna | : | How can the trees bear the rotis? This is not written in our books. |
| Babaji | : | Yes, my child, the trees can ... if you know how to generate, it is possible. |
| Muna | : | (Arguing) how can it be? (To the Guruji) Do you believe it? |
| Guruji | : | 1947, help him understand. |
| Swadhin | : | (Like a machine) "Don't ask; answer us what you are asked." |

| | | |
|---|---|---|
| Muna | : | Our dog Tommy does not ask us anything. I ask my dad and mom many questions. Mom gets angry quickly. |
| Guruji | : | I am not your mom, 1984. |
| Muna | : | I don't like this number. You call me by my name, 'Muna'. |
| Guruji | : | Your society has given your name, but the party has given you a number here. |
| Muna | : | Why? |
| Guruji | : | Each one of us is a weapon, a bomb. The bombs are named after and counted with numbers. |
| Babaji | : | (being terrified) Bomb! |
| Guruji | : | All right! We are all a suicide squad to demolish and destroy the society. |
| Babaji | : | O *mahimāmaya paramapurusa*! Each one of them is a bomb! Where have you sent me? Where is the group of four trees? Where is that flute's magical and charming sound? |
| Swadhin | : | I am leading you there. |
| Babaji | : | Lead, O God, guide me! Could you not put me with the bombs? |
| Swadhin | : | That was my house, Guruji, before I joined the party. |
| Babaji | : | And the player of the flute? |
| Swadhin | : | Before I joined the party, he was my father. I am Swadhin. |
| Muna | : | (Innocently) Who is your father now? |
| Swadhin | : | (Like a machine) "Don't ask me anything…", 1984. |

An Uninhabited Forest | 99

| | | |
|---|---|---|
| Muna | : | You are talking like my father- this is my new car; that is my old one. |
| Babaji | : | Nice! Very nice!! |
| Guruji | : | Parents, brothers and sisters, sons and daughters- nobody is at the party. All are friends, only friends. |
| Babaji | : | Very nice! Very nice! The world is full of friends. |
| Swadhin | : | My father…I mean to say Banshidhar is ill-tempered if he obstructs our movement towards the trees. |
| Babaji | : | Impossible. I told them to have food after washing off my body. Banshidhar must be waiting for me. I am a holy man or religious guest, *ha…ha…ha*! He must have been waiting for me for years. |
| Swadhin | : | You have not washed off your body, Swamiji. |
| Babaji | : | Food is prohibited if I have not cleaned myself. Consuming roti is forbidden, but roti-donating is an excellent work, my child. Come with me. |
| Guruji | : | Then you all proceed; march ahead! |
| Muna | : | Do I? |
| Babaji | : | Yes, my child- from the children to the older men and women (If any). [They all march ahead. Babaji walks in his unique dancing style. Swadhin stands facing the others.] |
| Swadhin | : | You must remember a small point. I have known Banshidhar since my birth. Banshidhar gets annoyed |

| | | |
|---|---|---|
| | | if all say something at a time (simultaneously). |
| Guruji | : | I will say I am the leader of the party. |
| Babaji | : | I am an incarnation of the *Dharma*. I will say. I have been ordered in the dream to say- The place where the flute's music will be heard in the middle of the dense forest; God will appear there through my voice. |
| Guruji | : | The, let's cast our votes. |
| Swadhin | : | (Like a machine) "What Guruji does is right." |
| Babaji | : | *Ha...ha...ha*! Alas! Guruji has told me to put you in the vote box. O Madhav! O Madhusudan!! It was an unjust time! |
| Guruji | : | We are ruined; we have nothing to donate but votes. We must avail that facility, Babaji. |
| Babaji | : | O stupid! Say 'Swamiji'! |
| Guruji | : | Don't deprive us of that. That is our right. |
| Babaji | : | Right?   O God! Whether party or Dharma is great? |
| Muna | : | What is dharma, Swamiji? |
| Babaji | : | (Shaking his chin) Alas! How innocent you are! How innocent you are in your way of uttering the word 'Swamiji' from your tiny lips! Nice! You are a kid; how can I help you understand the word so quickly, my child... (Showing himself) The person who stays closer to virtuous people is your |

|  |  |  |
|---|---|---|
|  |  | Babaji Uncle. |
| Guruji | : | 1984! Listen to me… |
| Muna | : | How often will I tell you? My name is Muna. My good name is Mukti Das, my father's name is Jagat Das, and my mother's is Dharitri Das. |
| Babaji | : | Wonderful! Mukti and Das. |
| Guruji | : | The meeting on internal matters will be held later. Without any delay, roti… |
| Babaji | : | In Sal Tree two, in Mango Tree two, in Neem Tree two, in Tamarind two… (Counting) |
| Muna | : | Tamarind Tree? We generally store tamarinds in jars. |
| Babaji | : | Trees are tied to the bottles. Once you see it, you will know. |
| Muna | : | (Crying, marching ahead) I will see the trees first, I will see the trees… [Muna walks first. Others follow him as if the primitive people quest for prey or are in the forage. After covering some distance.] |
| Guruji | : | 1947! (All stop.) I can't walk anymore. |
| Swadhin | : | We have no insulin with us right now. Our stock is over. |
| Guruji | : | Hold me; carry me over your shoulder. [As Vikramaditya carried over his shoulder vampire, Swadhin carried over Guruji. Swadhin has not taken Guruji to his shoulder, but Guruji jumps over to his shoulder in an attempt like a vampire.] |

| | | |
|---|---|---|
| Guruji | : | Take me with you, take me with you... call while marching ahead... |
| Swadhin | : | O Madhav! Tornado will rise! The leader sits on Swadhin's shoulder. Dharma is walking alone! Mukti, can you allow me to sit on your shoulder? |
| Muna | : | Swamiji, I to you on my shoulder? |
| Babaji | : | Okay, let me not sit. Time has changed. (saying to himself) they will be set right if I build a temple. I will see the spot after reaching. |
| Guruji | : | Are you jealous of me, Swamiji? Nobody is here to shoulder you. |
| Babaji | : | (Saying to himself) I will sit upon your shoulder once the temple is built. Rascal, you are sitting like a vampire. |
| Swadhin | : | (Like a machine) "Guruji is our Netaji/leader; he can see everything." |
| Guruji | : | Body, Mind, internal and external world. |
| Babaji | : | (Afraid of) what! |
| Swadhin | : | March ahead without any second thought, arrive at the Tree spot. |
| Muna | : | I will see the trees, Swami. I have read the books and seen the photos, but I have never seen the trees thoroughly. |
| Babaji | : | (Spontaneously) You also want to see fat trees... (He stops.) |
| Muna | : | What do you say, Swamiji? |
| Babaji | : | No, no, I said you to sing the song... (Starting with his style of singing the hymns) Twinkle, twinkle, little star, how I wonder what you are! |

[Muna sings in his style. Like a troupe of travellers doing a procession, they have left from left side to right side. Swadhin howls, "*huke ho, huke ho*", until he goes out of sight. The light gets dimmed.

Banshidhar comes from the audience's left side when the stage lights are on. He is alone. The trees also walk following Banshidhar's rhythm of movement from the right side and get fixed at their positions. Immediately after their reach, a green atmosphere is created again through the arrangement of different lights. Many things are still dim, dirty, and smoky. After this, until the end of the play, the characters' acting will be normal and daily based. From the background, the following stanza is heard intelligibly with a level tone in unison.]

| | |
|---|---|
| Stanza | : O Brother! Have you ever seen a forest where no human beings reside? |

[Banshidhar, disappointed, comes slowly and sits under the mango tree.]

| | |
|---|---|
| Neem | : *manisa bhāi* is disheartened. |
| Tamarind | : He is sitting silently. |
| Sal | : He does not look at us. |
| Mango | : He does not look at his front or back. |
| Neem | : He is neither smiling nor crying. |
| Tamarind | : Two moved but returned alone. |
| Sal | : Friend! then his wife perhaps… |
| Tamarind | : Don't say so, Buddy. She likes me very |

|  |  |
|---|---|
| | much. When she was pregnant, I gave her my fruits secretly. |
| Mango | : Let's ask him where she has gone. |
| Neem | : If he gets angry? |
| Sal | : Why will he be angry? |
| Neem | : If he cries? |
| Tamarind | : If he cries, I will help him laugh. |
| Mango | : How? |
| Tamarind | : I will drop my fruits; he will call Bishakha here to have the tamarind fruits…(Calling) *manisa bhāi*! |
| Banshidhar | : (Looking at them differently) What happened? |
| Banshidhar | : (Shouting immediately) O Bishakha… (waiting for a while) Bishakha? (To the tree) you take back your fruits. Who will eat? One who would eat… [He covers his face with a towel.] |
| Sal | : Is she not here? |
| Banshidhar | : Yes, it has already been two days. [Echo in Tree-voice: "How? How? How?"] |
| Banshidhar | : How did it happen? As usual, she left the world suddenly. You can't move, what will I tell you? (Showing) On that side, at a long distance from here, lies the *Nāndimundi* mountain. The top of the mountain is bald, while its foot is crowded with herbs, shrubs, and trees: Arka, Tulsi, dry ginger, long pepper, black pepper, cinnamon, thorn apple plant, etc., when she was breathless due to Asthma, I took her to |

*Nāndimundi* Goddess there.
[While saying, Banshidhar moves to the left side screen of the audience.]

Banshidhar : A small distance to cover...can't you? (Extending hand to inside) get hold of me.
[Holding Banshidhar's hands from that side, Bishakha comes bending down.]

Banshidhar : All medicines for your disease are available here. Medicine is also here in this wind. If you breathe here for a while, you will also be set right and feel energetic. Inhale the air slowly... exhale...inhale again...
[Bishakha tries hard but can't control her breathing-in and breathing-out process. She only becomes breathless.]

Banshidhar : Sit down here. I request milk from the Arka plant.
[Bishakha can't sit due to the critical condition of Asthma and bends down. She seems to be a four-legged creature.]

Banshidhar : O Goddess *Nāndimundi*! I say *Juhāra* to you, Goddess! I have brought your daughter to you. You help her live and bless my family, too.
[While Banshidhar says *Juhāra* to Goddess, Bishakha also says *Juhāra* to Her, with difficulty.]

Banshidhar : There were many plants here. Where are they now? Where is Arka, where

| | | |
|---|---|---|
| | | is Tulsi, where is the thorn apple plant? (Having seen) There is Arka... (Happily) I got.<br>[Going to the side-screens] |
| Banshidhar | : | O plant, give us the milk...<br>[One branch of the Arka plant falls; Banshidhar fails to squeeze that.] |
| Banshidhar | : | What's this? There is no milk from this branch. When we touched it earlier, milk dropped from its branches. (Holding the branch) Are you angry with me? Plant, are you angry with a man? I will make medicine, give me some drops of your milk. (To Bishakha) open your mouth...fresh milk will work. (Consoling himself) I know its fresh milk will also be effective.<br>[When Bishakha opens her mouth, Banshidhar tries to put a drop of Arka milk there, but there is no milk. Bishakha becomes breathless with a hissing sound. She grabs Banshidhar's towel closely. Her mouth is open.] |
| Banshidhar | : | Don't behave like this, Bishakha! O Goddess *Nāndimundi*! Who is that rascal who uproots the plants from your surface/land? I will kill him. You, all rascals, fraudsters! You will chop the plants and sell the milk filling in the bottles. You will build your society there, here, my Bishakha...? She looks at you with hope. My Lalita died |

because of the British Government; can't my government save my Bishakha's life? You stay here; I watch now who will steal from the jungle surreptitiously...
[When he gets up saying so, his towel tightly clutched in the hands of dead Bishakha. While standing, Banshidhar's saffron towel, white dhoti, and Bishakha's green saree give the impression of an Indian Tricolour (flag); with a classical note, the following stanza is heard.]

Stanza : Have you seen a forest where no trees reside?
[Banshidhar slowly sits and looks at Bishakha. The voice of the mouth organ playing 'twinkle, twinkle' is heard at a distance.]

Banshidhar : (hearing the sound) The thieves have reached here, Bishakha. If they don't get anything, they will look upon this dead body. The White Government pulled your elder sister when she was alive; I won't allow these fellows even to touch your dead body. We will leave this place. I will take you to our place. There I will, to your dead body...dead body? Where will I get wood?
[Banshidhar can't pick up Bishakha's dead body but pulls. The stage lights are off for a moment.]
[After the lights are on, Banshidhar

|  |  |
|---|---|
| | stands in the same place where he was talking. He is crying, covering his face with the towel.] |
| Tamarind | : *manisaa bhāi*! |
| Banshidhar | : You can take back your fruits. (Showing a palm full of tamarinds) Tamarind Tree. |
| Tamarind | : We only serve or give, *manisaa bhāi*! [Tree-song] |
| Song | : *manisaa bhāi*! *manisaa bhāi*! We are destined not to take back, *manisaa bhāi*! *manisaa bhāi*! We are born to give. [Tree-song diminishes.] |
| Banshidhar | : My wife is lying there dead, Tree. If her dead body is not set on fire, ... [At a distance is heard "*huke ho, huke ho*"] |
| Banshidhar | : The wild animals will eat her away... (Crying) I am alone. I came and stayed alone; I can't fight with them. O Tree! Give me woods; I will set her dead body on fire, otherwise she... (crying naturally) *ho...ho...ho...* |
| Neem | : Don't cry, *manisaa bhāi*, take now. |
| Banshidhar | : Give...give...(gratefully) let her save from the jackals, vultures, and wild creatures. [putting the flute on the ground, he requests.] [Echoe in Tree-voice: "Take... take... take"] |
| Banshidhar | : Saying *Juhār* while removing the welled-up tears from his eyes. Yes... |

An Uninhabited Forest | 109

|  |  |
|---|---|
|  | yes...Rama Kaka, Shama Bhai, my *Sunanaki*, O Brother, you give...give... [From the trees, the branches immediately fall one after one as if they were their hands. Nearby is heard a "Twinkle, twinkle" voice through the mouth organ.] |
| Banshidhar | : That voice...that thief. Before that, I will free you, Bishakha. [As the mouth organ's voice comes closer, Banshidhar gathers wood fast and places it on the left screen.] |
| Mango | : You also take me with you, *manisaa bhāi*! [Banshidhar leaves.] |
| Tamarind | : Neem, you see. *manisaa bhāi* can't drag his wife's dead body. |
| Sal | : Maybe, her weight has increased. |
| Tamarind | : Who knows, but our weight will be reduced after death. |
| Neem | : Behold there, Neem! He will set her dead body on fire. |
| Sal | : They do that. |
| Mango | : What will be after her dead body is burnt? |
| Neem | : O stupid! What will happen? What happens to us- Ashes. |
| Tamarind | : After that, ashes will be mingled with soil. |
| Mango | : O, after death, we are all the same. |
| Sal | : Who is coming from this side? |
| Tamarind | : A man? |

| | | |
|---|---|---|
| Mango | : | Other human beings are here with a kid. Who is that ascetic one? |
| Neem | : | (looking at Muna) Oh My God! A small kid!<br>[Muna, Swadhin, Guruji, and Babaji enter from the right side on his shoulder.] |
| Babaji | : | Cent per cent here. Excellent, very nice! |
| Muna | : | Ouch! What tree is it, Swami? And, what's that tree? |
| Babaji | : | Mango, Sal, Neem, Tamarind- all are here together. |
| Muna | : | (Clasping the Mango Tree) Very lovely! |
| Swadhin | : | Guruji! Please get down.<br>[Without Swadhin's help, Guruji, like a vampire, jumps and stands up with a staff.] |
| Guruji | : | If we don't get *rotis* here, I will sit on your shoulder again, 1947. Again, you will carry me over to another place. |
| Swadhin | : | "What Guruji does is right." |
| Guruji | : | Then Swami? |
| Babaji | : | Yes, you will get rotis Guruji. (To himself) You will eat rotis as round as the moon. |
| Muna | : | Where? The trees don't bear rotis. |
| Babaji | : | God's decree in dream will never be wrong, for he is the cause of everything in the world! O Banshidhar, please let me hear your playing of the flute. |
| Swadhin | : | (Calling) Banshidhar! Bishakha! The |

|         |   |                                                                                                                                                                                                                          |
|---------|---|--------------------------------------------------------------------------------------------------------------------------------------------------------------------------------------------------------------------------|
|         |   | older man and woman will flog me. (To Babaji) leave it! Let them die! Swami! You help the trees bear rotis.                                                                                                              |
| Babaji  | : | Have I yet to tell you the place where the trees will bear rotis? Will it be with playing the flute's magical note?                                                                                                      |
| Swadhin | : | Help the trees bear rotis without any delay. I am playing the flute. Here is the flute… [Babaji falsely closes his eyes. Swadhin plays the flute. An extraordinary, bad voice comes out of the flute. Babaji gets soon terrified.] |
| Babaji  | : | Stop! Stop!! [Swadhin stops playing the flute.]                                                                                                                                                                           |
| Babaji  | : | Hello, what's your number? Are you playing the flute or doing something else? Do you have any stomach problems? Here, it's a holy place.                                                                                 |
| Swadhin | : | I have not had anything, Swami. My stomach is slightly…                                                                                                                                                                  |
| Babaji  | : | Slightly? (suddenly with an ascetic look) God, himself has told the trees can bear roti only where the flute's sweet, resonant, and charming voice will be heard. If the trees listen to your playing of the flute, they will fly. Where will the rotis be born? |
| Guruji  | : | How far?                                                                                                                                                                                                                 |
| Babaji  | : | That magical flute is the only option.                                                                                                                                                                                   |
| Swadhin | : | Banshidhar is not here…(Calling) Banshidhar! Banshidhar! (Having seen the branches of Mango Tree) Oh!                                                                                                                     |

| | | |
|---|---|---|
| Guruji | : | Well! (Seeing) branches? |
| Babaji | : | (Seeing the tree) this story! |
| Swadhin | : | But where did the two move? |
| Babaji | : | Where will they go? Both have gone to the market for selling the firewood. [Swadhin stands still at the place where the small axe was buried. He confirms that the axe is in the right place.] |
| Swadhin | : | All right. Had he been here, he would not have allowed me to enter. He is not my father but a mischievous fellow. I have helped him understand repeatedly- Cut down the trees, sell the wood, and build a house for us. He didn't listen to me. At last, he did what I had told him before. Babu Banshidhar! Why were you annoyed with me at that time? You told, "I won't cut down the trees. I will never allow others. These are not the fruit trees. The trees bear 'gold'." |
| Muna | : | Which tree bears 'gold', Uncle? |
| Guruji | : | Not uncle, 1947. |
| Muna | : | I will call him 'Uncle', Grandpa. |
| Guruji | : | (Angrily) No… |
| Muna | : | (With obstinacy) Yes, I will. Which tree bears 'gold', Grandpa? |
| Babaji | : | If you know how to cut down the trees, every tree will offer you 'gold', my dear. |
| Muna | : | But why will you cut down the trees? |
| Babaji | : | For hoarding gold. A hut will be made |

|  |  |
|---|---|
|  | from the cut-down trees. If I sit in that hut, it will be regarded as the temple. My disciples will come and touch my feet to get my blessings. They will offer 'gold' to me. Gold can be available there by the people's donation, or we will purchase gold. |
| Muna | : What will you do with "gold", Swami? You are an ascetic! |
| Babaji | : All right. I am utterly an ascetic, but others need gold. O Madhav! O Swarnamaya Madhusudan! |
| Muna | : My mom is with a considerable amount of gold. |
| Guruji | : You are denied not to say anything about your home. |
| Muna | : Why can't I say, Grandpa? |
| Guruji | : I am not your grandpa. That's all. |
| Muna | : As I have no grandpa, I am saying so. |
| Swadhin | : Don't be obstinate, my little star. |
| Muna | : I recollect my mom's story. She must be crying day and night.<br>[Guruji and Swadhin look at each other.] |
| Muna | : You called me from the school and said my mom was serious. Again, you told me that my father had sent the car to pick me up. You didn't allow me to ring my parents. You brought me to the jungle and kept me starved.<br>[He reverses his suit's pocket and gets some remnants of the mixture] |

| | | |
|---|---|---|
| Muna | : | See, my friend Goldy offered me the mixture. It is over. What will I do here now? |
| Guruji | : | Your father delivers lectures on the 'Forest' in T. V. (teasing). You will do the plantation here. Your father will come to watch this. |
| Muna | : | If I plant, how will it benefit me? (To Babaji) You are saying to cut down the trees, Swamiji! |
| Babaji | : | (With solemnity) If God wants? God has ordered me in the dream. |
| Guruji | : | (Seriously, completing the sentence) Swamiji, by your charisma, show us the trees bear rotis. |
| Babaji | : | Well, first, you touch my feet.<br>[Both look at each other; Guruji hesitantly touches Babaji's feet.] |
| Babaji | : | Live long. But my child, you will think of your body later, first soul. God said- |
| Swadhin | : | (Completing the sentence seriously) I will reside where a dense forest is. |
| Babaji | : | The trees will bear roti, and my temple will be built there. |
| Swadhin | : | Have you seen new dreams like this, Swamiji? |
| Babaji | : | Yes, my child! I see new dreams every day, O Madhav! |
| Swadhin | : | When? After we met, you had not bathed, taken food, and slept. When did you see the dreams? |
| Babaji | : | I am *dharma*. I can say when, where, and with whom I am awake or slept |

## An Uninhabited Forest | 115

|          |   |                                                                                                 |
|----------|---|-------------------------------------------------------------------------------------------------|
|          |   | in my land (India). O Lord of the Universe, Motherland is greater and sweeter than heaven!      |
| Guruji   | : | You are telling lies to deceive us.                                                             |
| Babaji   | : | ha…ha…ha! I am *Siddha purusa*, my child!                                                       |
| Swadhin  | : | So what?                                                                                        |
| Babaji   | : | I will speak only the truth. I won't tell you anything else.                                    |
| Swadhin  | : | Then, is it true that the trees can bear rotis?                                                 |
| Guruji   | : | Our party demands rotis from the trees.                                                         |
| Babaji   | : | (Avoiding) Where, in the scriptures, is it written that I will always speak the truth, Guruji? Whether in the political books or religious scriptures? |
| Swadhin  | : | Oh! *Dharma, dharma, dharma*! What will one get from that '*dharma*'?                           |
| Babaji   | : | What will you get from '*huke ho* (howling)', my child?                                         |
| Guruji   | : | Had you told us about 'dharma' and 'temple' earlier, our party would not have come with you.    |
| Babaji   | : | 'Temple' is the other name of 'Roti', my child.                                                 |
| Muna     | : | (innocently) No temples are here.                                                               |
| Babaji   | : | As there is no temple here, it will be built.                                                   |
| Swadhin  | : | What do you want to say?                                                                        |
| Babaji   | : | I don't want to say anything; I am only a means. Lord said, "Temple is the name of the rotis' unending mountain. |

|  |  |
|---|---|
| | The forest of the mountain is with roti-bearing trees." |
| Swadhin | : What is this, Guruji? I am hungry now, and this boy… |
| Muna | : And so am I, Uncle. |
| Guruji | : Swami, you carry on. |
| Babaji | : Once the temple is built, everything will be available. All of us will benefit. |
| Guruji | : My benefit? |
| Babaji | : You will hide there. The Police will watch you patrolling outside. You will get everything without spending a little. There will be no need to hide in the hilly tract. Inside the temple, you may get everything you will search for, maybe, the country, foreign land, roti, medicine for diabetes, etc. |
| Swadhin | : My benefit? |
| Babaji | : You will be immensely benefitted, my unemployed child. If you worship, hold the temple's flag, beat the drum, or show the way to the pilgrims by waving your hands as a tourist guide or beating the pilgrims, you will get benefits only. |
| Guruji | : And of a new number? |
| Muna | : I don't need anything, Swamiji. |
| Babaji | : I need. |
| Muna | : (Clasping a tree) I will go home. |
| Guruji | : This is your home. |
| Muna | : This is a jungle. |
| Swadhin | : A house will be built after we cut down the trees. |

| | | |
|---|---|---|
| Muna | : | (Clasping like that) Will it be cut down? |
| Babaji | : | After that, you will be within my ambit. You will know the religious rites. You will benefit from that…then, all will benefit from the temple, O Madhav Madhusudan! |
| Muna | : | How will you benefit, Swamiji? |
| Babaji | : | Ha…ha…ha! If the world gets benefitted, I will earn money and wealth. I am an ascetic. |
| | | [Muna learns slowly as the bud blooms into a flower.] |
| Babaji | : | All have agreed to cut down the trees, O Madhav Madhusudan! |
| | | [Guruji and Swadhin nod like two toys running by the springs.] |
| Babaji | : | You? |
| | | [Muna is caressing a tree.] |
| Babaji | : | (Egoistically) We will cut down this tree fast. Okay, all right, my child, we will keep up your words. How will we cut down? Where is the weapon? |
| | | [Guruji brings out a pistol from the pre-independent era from the inner pocket of his sweater.] |
| Guruji | : | Yes! |
| Swadhin | : | Pistol, Guruji? |
| Muna | : | (Cowardly) What will you do with the pistol, grandpa? |
| Babaji | : | We will cut down the trees, Guruji! Will we do so by the pistol? Stop your gun… |

| | | |
|---|---|---|
| Guruji | : | If it is fired, only you will hear the sound, Swamiji. If a bullet comes out of the gunpoint, that hints at the revolutionary slogan. Isn't it, 1947? |
| Swadhin | : | (Like a machine) "What Guruji does is right." |
| Guruji | : | (Like a machine) "Guruji is our leader (Netaji). He is watching all this." (Normally) internal and external, front and back, past and future ... |
| Babaji | : | Then, both you and I are equal, my friend. I can also see internal and external... (Showing pistol) what's inside it? |
| Guruji | : | Bullet of freedom |
| Tamarind | : | This is the gun factory. |
| Sal | : | Mango, only man makes guns. |
| Mango | : | Neem, my friend, they won't get food to eat! |
| Neem | : | They may or may not get food to eat but fire guns. |
| Tamarind | : | Let them fire the guns. They can't harm us. |
| Swadhin | : | The trees won't be cut by the gun's firing...hold on... [Swadhin brings out the small axe buried under the ground and smiles at discovering something new.] |
| Swadhin | : | *Ha...ha...ha...* (Smiling) |
| Guruji | : | (Imitating him) *hi...hi...hi...*(Smiling) |
| Babaji | : | Alas! Alas!! |
| Muna | : | (Clasping the tree nervously) *he...he...he...* |

| | | |
|---|---|---|
| Swadhin | : | (Sarcastically) Banshidhar thought, "Swadhin doesn't know where the axe is. Once, he said, you must stand on your legs and work on your own; your hand will be the weapon; when you can't, I will give you a weapon. You will protect yourself by bringing out the weapon and saving the world. But you won't kill the animals, cut down the trees, but to yourself? What will you do to yourself?" |
| Babaji | : | To protect yourself, O Banshidhar's son! |
| Guruji | : | Yes!<br>[Guruji unloads the bullet from the pistol and throws it away. The bullets are dispersed.] |
| Babaji | : | Then, Let Lord Ganesh be invoked first…Delay is dangerous. Isn't it?<br>[All three move to the tree that Muna clasps.] |
| Sal | : | Let them chop me first; you live, Mango, because you are the king of fruits. |
| Mango | : | Let them chop me first; you live, Neem, because you are the king of medicines. |
| Neem | : | Let them chop me first; you live, Tamarind, because you benefit all. |
| Tamarind | : | Let them chop me first; you live, Sal, because you are the tallest tree for which the forest exists.<br>[While smiling, all three march ahead.] |
| Muna | : | Grandpa! |

| | | |
|---|---|---|
| Sal | : | They… |
| Mango | : | What are they doing? |
| Neem | : | They… |
| Tamarind | : | Do they know… |
| Trees | : | God the Almighty? |
| Muna | : | Swamiji, Uncle… please, don't come … |
| Guruji | : | This is the party's work, 1984. Who is Grandpa here? |
| Babaji | : | Who is Swamiji? |
| Swadhin | : | Who is uncle here? |
| Babaji | : | *Kuruksetre dharmakshetre* (the great battlefield for the Mahabharat war between Kauravs and Pandavs). Arjun also asked this, my child. |
| Muna | : | I am not Arjun, Swamiji. I am a small kid…Mukti Das. |
| Babaji | : | The war of righteousness, my child…a war here for freedom, salvation, and protection. |
| Guruji | : | One agenda activity |
| Babaji | : | A temple will be built; gold will be in the temple. |
| Swadhin | : | Unemployment will vanish. |
| Guruji | : | People will get roti (food). |
| Muna | : | Only trees can bear roti? Without them, how can we get roti? |
| Swadhin | : | Not in the trees but on the temple's walls, little star! |
| Muna | : | You cheat me, you are telling lies… liars! |
| Three of them | : | Move away… |
| Muna | : | (Shouting with obstinacy) No… |

## An Uninhabited Forest | 121

| | | |
|---|---|---|
| | | [Echo in Tree-voice: "No...no...no...no..."] |
| Muna | : | (With the same rhythm as the tree voice) Please, don't come. I will see the trees and show my children while growing up. |
| Babaji | : | Farsightedness! Nice! Very nice!! |
| Guruji | : | He won't listen to us like this. |
| Swadhin | : | He is a public school student trying to be smart! (Raising the small axe) ...! |
| Guruji | : | Go ahead, 1947... |
| Muna | : | What are you saying, Guruji? |
| Swadhin | : | Go away... (like a machine) "Don't ask me anything..." |
| Babaji | : | It's the auspicious time to proceed, my child. |
| Swadhin | : | Go away... |
| Muna | : | What do you say, Uncle? |
| Guruji | : | Your party supports you. |
| Babaji | : | Religion supports you...move ahead! |
| Muna | : | Where is 'dharma'? Where? |
| Swadhin | : | Here... |
| | | [Swadhin stabs or chops one tree.] |
| Muna | : | (Shouting) No... |
| | | [Muna clasps that tree.] |
| Tree-Cry | : | No...no...no... |
| Swadhin | : | See the magic of the weapon, Muna. [Swadhin chops trees one by one. The mournful voice of the trees is heard in each axing. Muna clasps every hurt-stabbed tree.] |
| Muna | : | You don't know what you are doing... (Crying) Don't chop them, Uncle. |

| | | |
|---|---|---|
| Guruji | : | They don't die; they are getting martyred on the revolutionary path. |
| Muna | : | It is written in the books, and our sir says the trees have their own lives. |
| Guruji | : | I am your Guruji. |
| Muna | : | They have their own lives, Guruji. |
| Babaji | : | Had they had tongues, they would have lived, my child…(touching the chin)…go away… |
| Guruji | : | Go away, 1984. |
| Muna | : | (Standing upright, courageously) My name is Mukti Das. I am a human, not the designated number of your deceitful group. I won't move from here (extending his hands), do what you want. (Clasping a tree) do…cut me into pieces… |
| Swadhin | : | Your fate! (Roaring) *huke ho*! [While Swadhin raises his small axe to cut down the tree Muna has clasped, Banshidhar reaches there holding a firebrand. His eyes are burning more brightly than the fire. His body and dhoti are irregularly spotted with black.] |
| Banshidhar | : | Nobody can touch the trees. [Wind sings sweetly as if the trees breathe happily in consolation.] |
| Banshidhar's tone | : | Your small axe is stolen, Banshidhar. |
| Banshidhar | : | Not the tiny axe; I need a light; I will destroy. |
| Swadhin | : | (Cowardly) Dad! |
| Banshidhar | : | I am only Banshidhar. |

| | | |
|---|---|---|
| Swadhin | : | (While going, calling) Mom! |
| Banshidhar | : | (Standing in the front) Your mom's funeral pyre...he is inhuman...come...can you control yourself? Hold...come, who is coming, come...I have not ended my fighting...come... |
| Muna | : | Why don't you come? Come... (removing tears) Come, Religion/Dharma! Party, you come on, hit me! Come on, You liars, fraudsters...hit me! Party, dharma! |

[When Banshidhar steps forward, these three move backward.]

| | | |
|---|---|---|
| Banshidhar | : | Locusts! Parasites!! First forest, then human beings, then party, then dharma. Go to that forest where I won't be...Banshidhar won't be there...humans won't be there. (Shaking the *maśāl*/light) Go now... |
| Muna | : | Go...get lost! |
| Guruji | : | Carry the vampire over your shoulder, 1947. |

[Guruji, as earlier climbs on Swadhin's shoulder.]

| | | |
|---|---|---|
| Swadhin | : | (Like a machine) "What Guruji does is right." |
| Muna | : | Is he right? |
| Babaji | : | God orders me to leave the place in the dream, O Madhav Madhusudan! |
| Guruji | : | Let's search for that place where we will get 'roti'. |
| Babaji | : | Where a temple will be built; there we will get 'roti'. |

| | | |
|---|---|---|
| Guruji | : | Let's go… |
| Swadhin | : | *Huke ho, huke ho!* |
| | | [They leave the place.] |
| Banshidhar | : | (To the trees) You were all right. Even God does not know what the human children will be in the future. He is now a jackal… |
| Muna | : | (doubtfully) With whom do you converse? |
| Banshidhar | : | (Smiling slightly) I? |
| Muna | : | (moving to a distance) Are you like us? |
| Banshidhar | : | I am a human being, like you. They were vultures. Come to me, my dear. |
| Muna | : | I? |
| Banshidhar | : | (Showing the light/torch) Continue burning the light. When you can't work, you will hand it over to your son only for light. You won't listen to others' flattery or coaxing. Their words may be like the nectar, but being an ascetic and a politician, they will exploit others…yours, mine… (showing to the trees) theirs… (seeing, touching) much blood dripped, no more blood to be dripped… |
| Muna | : | I will go home, sir. |
| Banshidhar | : | Make home to the forest, my child, but don't make forest to the home… (handing the torch/light over to Muna) You watch here…holding the *maśāl*… (He leaves.) |
| Muna | : | Sir! Leaving me alone, you… |

| | | |
|---|---|---|
| Banshidhar | : | No, don't say alone... (showing the trees) Rama Kaka, Shama Bhai, Nani, and this Bhai are all with you. You are with them; they will talk to you, they will sing for you, they will help you in your sorrows and happiness, and the birds will also return to their nests here. |
| Muna | : | But where are you going, Sir? |
| Banshidhar | : | The fight does not end here. I must cover a long distance. Banshidhar must reach a new forest before they reach there. They will never find a forest where no human beings reside, being dishonest and quarrelsome until they breathe their last. Are you afraid of darkness? (Giving him the flute) play the flute...play, my child...darkness will be dispelled...Be Banshidhar... the eastern horizon will turn bright red before sunrise, and darkness will disappear.<br>[Muna holds the flute.] |
| Banshidhar | : | Let the entire forest be reverberated with the flute's musical cadence. Let me leave; I must cover a long distance. [Banshidhar marches ahead. Muna brings the flute to his lips. The tree song is heard with the flute's musical note.] |
| Song | : | Have you seen a forest where no human beings reside?<br>[Muna gets startled and looks at the |

trees happily. Banshidhar leaves. The sun rises amidst the flute's musical rhythm. The birds' chirping is heard along with the Tree song, the *'Surya Vandana'*.]

Surya Vandana : *"Tume Surya, Anshuman, Anshupati, Anshudhar.*
*Tume Rudra, Dinamani, Dinakara, Dibakara."*
[Muna does 'Surya Namaskar' and the screen drops down.]

**END**

**Black Eagle Books**

www.blackeaglebooks.org
info@blackeaglebooks.org

Black Eagle Books, an independent publisher, was founded as a nonprofit organization in April, 2019. It is our mission to connect and engage the Indian diaspora and the world at large with the best of works of world literature published on a collaborative platform, with special emphasis on foregrounding Contemporary Classics and New Writing.

www.ingramcontent.com/pod-product-compliance
Lightning Source LLC
Chambersburg PA
CBHW060614080526
44585CB00013B/831